■ General Introduction

Samuel Johnson noted as long ago as 1783 that 'All history was at first oral'. With this encouragement - if any was needed - the members of the Fenland Oral History Project class in Ely, led by Pam Blakeman as tutor, began to record their memories and reminiscences in the spring of 1996.

The Fenland Oral History Project was a four-year project, running from 1995 - 1999, through the University of Cambridge Board of Continuing Education. It was funded by the Higher Education Funding Council for England as part of their programme for widening the range and number of people participating in higher education. The project aimed to use oral history to demonstrate the agenda of adult education : classes where the student is central, where students' views and experience are valued and where students and tutor collaborate as equals in the business of teaching and learning.

Members of the Ely course talked of their childhood, of work and holidays, of celebrations and of death and of funerals, of their lives. They found much to say and derived pleasure and sometimes excitement from putting their memories onto audio-cassette. Less exciting, a task which called for considerable dedication, was the painstaking transcription of these tapes by members of the class. After this it was necessary to get the script typed - no small task, as much was handwritten at this stage, and without which editing would have been impossible. In fact, editing itself stimulated considerable discussion.

Voices of the Fens covers the oral history of a small area of the Black Fens and looks at some aspects of life in Ely, Soham and Littleport, as well as the surrounding villages. The memories of the oldest participants, May Turner and Phyllis Trevers, go back to their childhood in the early days of the twentieth century, and both mention the First World War. Other contributors bring the story up to date with reminiscences of the 1950s and '60s, and later, emphasising the importance of oral history as a source for understanding past experience. Participants came to realise that one can only truly begin to piece together an impression of the past by valuing all contributions equally : old and young, incomers and 'locals', urban and rural, from people from a wide variety of backgrounds and experience.

Pamela Blakeman
Ely
August 1998

GW00722493

Smells, fears, thrills, scares, sights and sounds

Terry Staines

When I first heard of this project, I wasn't exactly sure what was expected of us, so I used the procedure which we adopted at work in my later years which was brainstorming, so I put down the various headings and listed my own quick thoughts under those headings.

The first one was smells, my life seems to be a memory of smells, from my childhood when my father worked in the brewery, I would go and see him quite regularly, and there just outside the place that he worked was a pile of hot hops, usually steaming and they had a very, very unique smell all of their own, and I rather gather that after they had cooled off, on a Saturday morning the dray driver's job would be to go round and sell these by the load to people, who bought them to put on their allotments as green manure. There was a smell of beer and I was shown very often into the fermenting room where the brass vats stood. There was a smell of the dray horses themselves, horses always have their own, rather unique smell. The smell of burning wood as the cooper put the rings on the barrels, when the ring was red hot just before he hosed them down to make them contract on to the barrel. Also, the smell, the burnt smell of horse hoof at Brand's smithy. We used to come home from school and call in there very often to see the great shires being re-shod, and an odd smell that comes to mind was the smell of powdered egg, which was a wartime luxury as far as I am concerned, mix it with water, put in the pan and you got almost a pure egg pancake. Have that with some bread with some special margarine as it was known in the wartime, and I was anyone's.

The next heading I put down was my fears. When I was very young lad at Market Street school, I was really terrified of going by the green when the gypsies were there, selling their horses. I don't know

T. Staines - On the Beach

why. Someone had obviously told me something bad about gypsies and I went the long way round to avoid them. After my father died, I would be sent to my sister's, who lived between, in a village called Pennistone, which is between Sheffield and Blackpool, and for a day out I would catch a train to Barnsley. I can remember to this day being absolutely terrified by busloads of men with no eyes, they were simply all black with miners' hats and great big clogs on. I can remember being very, very frightened as I was chased across the King's school fields at the bottom of Barton fields, by Mr Bailey because we shouldn't have been there. He was the groundsman, he had a shotgun. We raced across the field and hid behind the metal or the - sorry, what am I talking about - the corrugated tin changing rooms and he let go a blast of his shotgun, and that led us even more [of a] dance, over the ditch in one [leap], through all the bushes and reeds, up over the railway gates and railway lines, across to the river, up to the Cutter and home via Silver Street and I don't think three Mr Baileys would have caught us that particular day.

Another heading I had was thrills. The first one I remember was being allowed to open the gates of the railway for Mr Garner who was the signalman, he didn't like going up and down the steps anyway. He allowed us to open the gates, we were also allowed to stand near his signal box and watch trains such as the Mallard come by. Cycling to Huntingdon to see trains was another thrill, cycling to Waterbeach to watch the first jets just after the war. Meteors etc were stationed there. Cycling to Cambridge for trainspotting, we were talking away quite happily, my friend and I - Michael Smith was his name - we were biking through Milton, we were looking at each other paying absolutely no attention, and luckily

for me, I was on the middle of the roadside and Michael was chatting away, didn't see a parked van and went head first straight through a back window and finished up in Addenbrooke's hospital, so we missed our trainspotting that day.

A particular thrill I can remember was going to my sister's, and her husband taking me to Blackpool to see Stanley Matthews playing football. We stood there for two and a half hours waiting for the game to start and about quarter hour before the kick off the ground filled up and I never did see Stanley Matthews, I saw nothing but the backs of people's jackets.

Scares that I can remember. I went with a friend to the sugar beet settling ponds. We were there to gather some rather nice smelling flowers, for his sister to make scent with, and we did this and we then got bored and we had got catapults with us, and we started to shoot stones at each other. We would run, run further and further away and eventually I got out of the cover of the trees, and I ran out of stones and my friend hadn't so he was allowed several free shots. I had to run further and further away and it seemed to be getting stickier as I ran along and of course, I had a rather large pair of Wellington boots on and eventually they would not come out of the mud and nor would I, and I started to settle, they were actually known as settling ponds and I know why.

I got down about as far as my waist, in about half an hour and the Page family, who I was quite accustomed to, they had also come down there to do some fishing and they clambered out to me by using empty crisp and biscuit tins on their feet and got some wood out to me and pulled me out and even went [back] to pull out my Wellington boots.

My friend, his sister and his mother, we went home and I think they all stood about ten yards away from me and I don't blame them, I was stood in the yard and Mrs Brown literally stripped me down there and then, took me up, stood me in the bath, hosed me down, made me have a complete bath, and by the time I got out, she'd got all of my stuff washed, dried and ironed and my mother never did know what I'd fallen into there.

The next heading I used was sights. The sight of cattle being driven along West Fen Road from Green's farm down to their grazing area in the fens towards Coveney. Also the cattle being driven from Runciman's farm, right opposite my mother's front door at 22 St John's Road, to their grazing further along St John's Road. Also, the sparks that flew from the fire at Brand's Smithy as he blew up the fire with the bellows.

Another sight I liked and enjoyed very much was watching a man called Bass pat one pound of butter, he would pat it up and wrap it up in about 50 seconds flat and I was never, never ever anything but amazed that they all came to the same weight. It was a master at work. There was the sight of the cattle market on

Thursday when I was a child. There would be bulls, heifers, horses, pigs and every sort of animal and bird up for sale. And it was just an amazing place to be, absolutely busy, full of people buying. Butchers going to the auctions to buy their own meat from the cattle ring, as they were paraded around.

Finally, I put down the heading of sounds. I can remember, I don't know the man's name, I can remember the "Oyez, oyez" of the Town Crier. He would come and stand outside Reeder's butcher shop at the end of St. John's Road, opposite to Fletcher's shop and call out his news and people would come from probably the first ten or fifteen houses [in] each of the three streets to hear the latest declaration. And I can remember the jingle, one of the first I'd ever heard in my life, from an ice-cream van, the firm was called Pocklington's. I can also remember the very faint sound of the handbell, I don't know who did this but someone stood on the corner of St John's Road and West End with a bicycle, in front of which there was a large box, and they would sell from that cream cheese, all laid out on straw platters and he announced his arrival with a handbell. I can remember that. "Powell's of Sutton". Oh, I see, yes.

T. Staines - Ely Brewery

▆▆▆▆ Childhood

Phyllis Trevers

When I was little there were no other children in my lane but if I wanted to play there were children in other streets. I remember that I was very ill once and was tubercular so my dad built me a shed outside. I used to sleep in it. I was able to get up and I went in this lane and one of the children offered me a bag. She said "Here's some sweets for you, Phyllis". When I took them and when I opened the bag they were black hodmidods - you know what I mean - snails. I liked living in my shed. I thought it was great. When I was thirteen and a half I left school because my (birthday) was during the summer holidays. My school was Little Downham Feoffees Mixed. When I was over the hedge in my shed lots of people came to see me, the teachers, the Finchams, old Mrs Crane and all of them came - they didn't worry about TB being catching. Then I had rheumatic fever.

Yes, I used to help clean the mangels. There was a great family called Harrison lived at Guild Acre farm and they used to run out in the fields without their shoes and socks. It was at the end of Little Downham on the road to Pymoor. Oh, yes, I did lots of potato picking and helped stack them all up and put them in clumps. You filled your basket and you stood it on the side and the cart came along and a man picked them up and threw them into the cart and then he took them to the heap. I also did onion wringing (wringing the tops of the onions). That made your hands sore. We earned 1/9d a night and we thought we were millionaires. I must have been about fourteen then. Oh, I might have been on a holiday - I should think I would be about 14.

Later on came sugar beet, didn't like sugar beet. There were lots more people employed when I was young than there are today. My brothers used to go where my dad worked or any other farmer and they could clean, the men I remember, a man at the top of our lane had a pig killed and you went up with lots of hot buckets of water, threw them over the pig and we went and scraped all the hairs off. I didn't mind doing that. It didn't put me off pork. I didn't see that pig killed but I did see another one killed. They jabbed it in the throat - I didn't mind. My mum was a very good baker. That's how I got my tuition and she got it from her mother. When the harvest was on we had a donkey cart. After school mum used to take us out in the donkey cart. She had already made up my dad's 'foursies', we called it dockey in the morning and foursies at 4 o'clock, and she used to take us down to the field - I'm talking about the cornfield. Mum used to go and make the bands to put the sheaves in. Then we would help dad to stack them up - not always right. The sheaves were

Olive Staines and Edna Watson

stood up then made into stacks. it was lovely to be allowed to go up the stack. When that was all finished we used to take our chickens and they were put in the field to gather up all the corn. That was a good bit of help to our parents. At harvest time everybody helped. My mum used to make an oatmeal drink because my dad never had beer, I don't think he ever had a glass of beer. This oatmeal was sent down in stone jars with corks in. We were allowed to have a drop. My dad also had cold tea in one of these jars, the brewery had them. I've got one or two at home now.

One thing I remember about my father, when he was a boy, they used to go to these Election meetings and they used to take sparrows and tie ribbons on their legs and let them through the school room to upset the meetings. Nothing changes.

I had a pet rabbit. My dad had a potato clump and one day a terrible thing happened. Old Mr Crane's dog chased the rabbit around the potato clump and caught up with it and killed it. I can't remember what the rabbit's name was. I cried for hours.

Edna Nunn

When I was small we didn't even have a bathroom, when I was very tiny before I went to school, we were bathed in a circular bath in one of the small bedrooms, a tin bath. On a Friday night we stayed in it until the water got cold and then didn't want to come out. But I think I was about eight when my father fitted up a bathroom and my brother, although he was brain damaged, he had a natural ability with anything mechanical - cars that sort of thing - put in central heating. Bought all the stuff from Dimmock's scrapyard down by the river and he fitted up the most Heath Robinson - but it was central heating. That heated

water so from then on we had a bathroom and just occasionally the water was hot enough to have a bath. There was no mains water for years. I'd left home before we got mains water - it was from wells. We had two wells. If you can imagine what wells were like in the fens. [We had] a stone - very heavy porcelain filter - [which] stood about two foot high on the side and water from the wells was out into that. I think it was charcoal in it and that filtered some of the impurities out of the water. There was a tap at the bottom. We were allowed to drink that water but most of it was boiled first. The water was always very black in the fens. The village people at the time were using it from what we called 'the pit'. I've since understood that it was a sort of pond dug to get the clay out for building cottages. It was years before we got mains water in Pymoor.

We didn't play a great deal. I was never allowed to have friends in to play when my father was at home. I very early learned

T. Staines

8

to look at the calendar to see when he was out on business. That meant I could probably have a friend in to tea. Everyone had to work. The washer woman came each Monday to do the washing. We fed quite well behind the business I suppose. My childhood was also dominated by the fact that my brother had a frightful accident when he was fourteen and I was four. Which meant that he was seriously ill for a very long time and I at this stage lived in Cambridge with my mother to be near the Evelyn Nursing Home. The interesting thing was of course there was no National Health Insurance in those days and it was Crawford's Biscuit Factory that guaranteed the money to pay for his hospitalisation and for his private nurse. Mercifully he lived but slightly brain damaged, he dominated my childhood, this sick brother.

My mother was very asthmatic and we thought that cats and dogs would aggravate her asthma. We did have dogs but they were always kept outside, two dogs. They were kept outside in kennels, exercised, but never in the house. We also had cats to keep down the mice and they were kept outside. They slept in the wash house. We had two horses but these were working horses. They delivered the groceries in the winter up the river bank (the Hundred Foot Bank) when the cars couldn't get. I would ride these horses. I loved to sit on these great cart horses and ride them, and I loved to feed them. We also had chickens and I loved to feed the chickens. We had a huge garden - a very small lawn but a large fruit garden and vegetables. My father was into growing bulbs in rows across his vegetable garden because he was always trying to perpetuate a new strain of bulb. I loved gardening from a tiny child and I was always helping my mother and my aunt in the garden. We had mushrooms, mushrooms grew in the fields because of

the horses grazing. There was a blackberry hedge all round and I loved gathering the blackberries in the autumn. We had two walnut trees, lots of plum trees and a damson tree which had to be thrashed and I loved this time when we would go down and collect the damsons.

When he was married my brother told me that my father paid him twenty five shillings a week. That would be in 1936. I know my mother paid her weekly maid 12/6d and I know the washer woman who came for the whole of Monday got paid 5/-. She earned it. Mrs Whybrow lived in one of the tiny cottages along the Hundred Foot Bank. Her husband was a bargee and she went out doing washing. She came on a Monday to us. She arrived at about half past seven, by which time Rose would have lit the copper fire and the water would be heating up.

Yes. Over the weekend in the summer we children would be sent to collect sticks to keep the copper going. There would be a mangle, the dolly tub, a sink in the wash house - the blue bag - the bath with the blue in. Mrs Whybrow would emerge from a cloud of steam from the wash house to come in for a cup of tea. She always wore a large white apron tied at the back. She would stay and have dinner with us. During this time she would be hanging out the washing down the field. We had a small field at the back where the horses grazed. She would bring it all in and before she went home at about 4 o'clock she folded the washing. What happened when it was wet I can't remember but she coped with it so that it was ready for my aunt to iron it and Rose would iron it on Tuesday. It wasn't just family washing. We had a butcher's shop and in those days the meat came wrapped in what must have been old tablecloths or old white sheets and my father insisted that these were boiled every week until there wasn't a bloodstain on them. They were boiled and they were boiled and they were boiled! Their standard of hygiene of course was different but very rigid. He'd been trained in the butchery department of one of the company shops and really the hygiene was more strict than it is today.

Ann Powell

There were no holidays with pay for lorry drivers before the war. Sunday was the only day off and Boxing Day. We went to my grandparents at Little Downham for dinner (dinner at midday) most Sundays. Mum and Dad walked - pushing me in the pram, and later I had a fairy cycle - two wheels and no brakes and my sister was in the pram. Sometimes I rode on a seat in front of my father's bike. On the fairy cycle I would cover twice the distance racing ahead and turning back to meet them. We went down Downham Road past Raventree Drove, up the hill to the windmill - there was no concrete curb - a grass strip ran between the path and the road. In summer dog daisies and red clover grew either side of the path.

Butterflies scattered as I whizzed past and honey bees in the clover dive-bombed me when I disturbed them. Once I saw a stoat ripple ahead as I chased along. On the right, just before the Spade and Becket pub, the baulks, the remains of medieval fields and the footpath from Chettisham, on the left a row of giant elm trees called the Seven Sisters. Pedal, pedal up the hill, past the road to California and Cabbage Hole (really Cowbridge Hall), sharp right into Lawn Lane. On the left, across the field, Steven's House with its peculiar blinds, where my cousin was nursery nurse and occasionally I was taken to play with her charges. Grandma and Grandad Bidwell lived in the council houses on the left which were built between the wars. It had a small front garden, flowers and a path edged with the Rose of Sharon, alive with dung flies and old-fashioned pinks, which were really white, and gave off perfume. All council houses of that era seem to have had vast privet hedges, granddad's was a way above his head and three sumach trees graced a scrap of grass

Ann Powell - Ely Goods Office Staff

behind the house. No-one wasted land on lawns. These houses were built with an allotment-sized back garden where the man of the house was expected to keep the family in fresh vegetables. There was a wash house and a chuck-out lavatory. This was buried at the bottom of the garden and produced tomatoes par excellence - just like they still do in the Far East.

My grandparents were strict chapel - no work other than meals on Sunday. No unseemly playing out. After the meal the obligatory Sunday afternoon sleep and woebetide the child who disturbed them. I had to sit still and not fidget on the hard rexine sofa, under the clock, with Queen Victoria, on being told she was Queen, on one side and a Pear's soap beauty picking berries in a leafy lane on the other. A gruff "Hold your noise" greeted any movement. Behind the door hung the leather strop for grandfather's cut-throat razor and, somewhere along the line, I gathered it was used to control unruly children. This was purely hypothetical because nobody ever laid a finger on me, but I was very good at doing what I was told!

There were two button-back armchairs on either side of the fire. One of my aunts, who knitted socks on four steel needles, left her knitting on one of those and I plonked myself down on it. One needle embedded itself in my bottom and my mother nearly fainted pulling it out. When I read this to her yesterday she said it makes her feel like that every time she thinks about it. This was the kitchen/living room with a big table to sit round, the sofa, two chairs, a big kitchen range and a long table under the window covered in oilcloth to wash up on. Thick net curtains covered the window, although no one overlooked them, beyond the garden there was a pasture and open fen

but they liked privacy and their respectability.

Although they were strict chapel, my uncles enjoyed a certain amount of license. Their Sunday dinner was put on a plate for when they bundled in from the pub. It was difficult to reconcile this with the "Hold your noise" attitude, but then I wasn't a wage earner.

Margaret Springer
When I was a child we always had a cooked breakfast and my father cooked it on Sunday morning and burnt the sausages every Sunday. Apart from that lunch was always meat and two veg. and a stodgy pudding, quite often suet pudding with custard. I don't eat custard now, I never eat stodgy puddings and I hardly have meat and two veg. I actually like Indian food mostly or highly spiced food. I'll just say when we were talking about smells I can remember my mother boiling up the potato peels and mixing it with bran for the hens and really it was the most disgusting smell.

Terry Staines
Childhood for me meant living at home with my mother, my father, my sister and one of my brothers. Peter, my oldest brother, was in Germany with the RAF during the war, so I remember very little about him. I know he didn't drink, nor smoke and it was explained to me later that he swapped his cigarette and drink allowance for chocolate and most of this came home in parcels addressed to me. I also remember a model of a Spitfire carved from perspex and one of a Lancaster bomber carved from wood that were also sent to me. My sister Olive worked at the brewery and each day I would stand by Fletcher's door at his shop on the corner of St John's Road and wait for her to come home because she would then pick me up and ride me home on her

bike, or the seat of her bike. My brother Eric worked at Lemmon's butcher's shop and he and I shared a bedroom and a double bed.

My play area, such as it was, was in the area now known as St Ovin's Green, Mayfield Close and Walsingham Way. At that time there were no buildings beyond Hills Lane apart from a scout hut which is now gone and which stood at what is now 32 St Ovin's Green and the Co-op Dairy that stood in the field at the Coveney end of what is now St Ovin's Green. I remember that when the builders moved in to start work on St Ovin's Green they laid a narrow gauge track around the area that was to be grassed and fed supplies to the workers on big steel trolleys that were rolled down a ramp at the far end of the Green. At the weekend those same trolleys also ran lots of little boys around without the builders knowing it and one or two accidents occurred.

One of the members of the Home Guard section that my father was in, for some reason when I saw him in the street he would always give me threepenny piece. In the window of Mr Fletcher's shop for many weeks there was a barley sugar twist that also cost threepence. The money was no problem but my mother wouldn't let me have the necessary coupons from the ration book to get it. So on the day that sweet rationing ended I can remember distinctly sitting on Mr Fletcher's doorstep at seven o'clock in the morning waiting for him to open to make absolutely certain I got that barley sugar twist and I'm afraid I ate the lot myself.

We had a family allotment near to the old isolation hospital, behind the Tower hospital, and all the family would work on it in the busy times. My mother and I also worked for Mr Chester in his orchard that surrounded the old pits opposite to the

present Debden Green. Also we helped Matt Smith in his orchard at plum, gooseberry and currant picking time. This orchard was opposite what is now the Close and looked across the old airfield at Witchford, the RAF bomber base.

The air raid shelter opposite to the entrance to Chief's Street beside the main entry to Runciman's farm was a favourite place for us, similarly, we would play our games of war in and around the pillbox in the first road past Green's Farm on the Coveney Road.

Our St John's Road gang would have regular stone fights with the Chief's Street gang on a sort of home and away basis really. We'd go to Chief's Street for our war and they'd come to us for the next one and we'd continue these quite vicious things throwing stones at each other, or until either a window got broken, or a door got hit, someone got hurt, or an adult would chase us away. Somehow when we were children we would be away from our homes all day and no one thought anything of it. We would play in places such as Barton Fields, Roswell Pits, Cuckoo Bridge, Witchford Aerodrome and probably not return home until 5 o'clock for the daily meal.

I remember the meals had little variety, a meat pie would be followed by a fruit pie, stew and dumplings would be followed by dumplings and jam or treacle. Steamed meat pudding would be followed by steam jam pudding. Our Sundays the first item on the plate was always Yorkshire pudding - a piece of Yorkshire pudding with gravy. Mum would then take back all our plates and give us another piece of Yorkshire with the necessary vegetables and meat. This was presumably to fill us up so we didn't want too much.

The other memorable event were the Saturday afternoon trip to one of the cinemas. I had a shilling pocket money and that would get me into the cinema, a bag of fish and chips afterwards from Lancaster's and a penny bag of broken buns or cakes from Bonnet's shop. At the Rex and the Public Room you would only see the film but if you went to the Majestic, in the interval, Mr Smith [the manager] would come up on the stage and throw apples, pears, bags of crisps, anything for you to catch.

For me church meant Sunday school in the Methodist Chapel in Chapel Street. I would leave my house in the morning and go along to Chief's Street where a young lady called Audrey Trevers, who was my Sunday school teacher, would walk us to Sunday school. My first trip to a wedding was to my eldest brother's. He married a young lady who came from Edinburgh and that meant a fairly long trip on the train up to Edinburgh with my mother on the Flying Scotsman which in those days

would pass through Ely. And the wedding was at 8 o'clock at night which was a fairly traditional thing in those days and I was dressed up as a little page boy and I can only remember vaguely the service and the meal. I can remember very distinctly the noise of the accordions which were used at night.

Holidays were a rare thing. I would go to my grandfather and grandmother's house at Wells-on-Sea occasionally and I would stay with them and help out around the house and run down to the beach occasionally with my grandfather. Most of my time in the school holidays was spent swimming from the moment the swimming pool opened until the moment it closed at 9 o'clock at night, I would be there. The school holidays were not a good time for me. I can remember during one school holiday I was pulled in for a bath, stood in the tin bath and against it was the tin copper that was used for boiling the water and I put my backside onto that copper and jumped a bit, was told by my mother not to make a fuss and to sit down and I sat down in the bath and I thought I was sitting on the flannel and I kept pulling bits of this flannel off and unfortunately when I stood up it appeared that the flannel was my skin and it was almost three weeks before I was able to sit down properly again. Shopping was usually OK. I would go with my mother up into Ely and kick up hell's delight in Peacock's and Woolworth's with their wide aisles and wooden floors which were made to measure for a little boy with Blakey's on his shoes, but the dreaded one, the dreaded trip was to Cambridge about once every two months. And that was dreaded for two reasons, first of all I could never get there without being sick all over the bus, I never ever got beyond Milton and then unfortunately the worst part of all was to get out at New Square and be dragged along to a shop called Laurie and

Lilian Martin - Christmas 1946

McConnells. It was an awful shop, no more running about there, everyone just stared at you, it was like being in a tomb. But the day would be saved eventually because we would go to the Civic Restaurant after we had been to Laurie and McConnells and whatever the first course was that was totally irrelevant because it was always followed by chocolate pudding and chocolate sauce, which was something of rarity in those days.

Occasionally, I was sent to my aunt and uncle in Sheffield. I would have notices pinned to me, one would be sewn to my mac pocket which would say "put this boy off at Sheffield Central" and the other would say "if lost, deliver this boy to Mr & Mrs Hand, 110 Ranby Road, Eccleshall, Sheffield". I remember that distinctly as I had to learn it off by heart before I went. We would then either stay with my uncle or aunt or they in turn would take me another few miles up the road where I stayed with my sister and we would go rambling over the moors and go ferreting and chasing rabbits etc.

June Strawson

I was an only child and my parents were determined that I was not to be brought up as a spoiled only child and I was also encouraged right from a very early age to have as many friends as possible and to join things and at seven I joined the Brownies and this was the beginning of a long time connection with the Guiding movement in Littleport and then later on in other places. At seven I wasn't very large, of course, and I can remember I had a uniform and eventually, after a year or so, I became a 'sixer' and I was in charge, or so I thought, of six other children. And we had the most marvellous time at Brownies, we met in the Mission Room, as it was called, attached to the Independent Chapel and then in the summer we met at

Miss Martin's house and then in her garden. That was terrific, we would charge around and do all sorts of things in this lovely garden. From Brownies I progressed to Guides as usual and I was very fond of Guiding. We had quite a large company and it was wartime. Now we became very important people, or so we thought, because we collected, as Guides, the wastepaper. All the wastepaper that was collected in Littleport during the war from houses and shops was collected by the Guides. Now, we had a gentleman who worked for the Martin family and he drove the horse-float and we collected our paper and cardboard in the horse-float and it was stored in an old stable building. Well, we used to get absolutely filthy but we were doing our bit for the war effort so that was the Guides' share of it. This went on for several years and also, as time went on, I became a patrol leader and then at about the age of 15 I became something called a Company Leader. They don't have Company Leaders any more, but I was very, very proud of my three stripes because, as Company Leader, I had three stripes. The ultimate, I suppose, came - I think it was '45 or '46 - when there was an enormous gathering of Guides at Ely Cathedral and I was asked by my Guide Captain and by the County Commissioner if I would be aide-de-camp, I think she called it, to Lady Baden-Powell for one day. That was the highlight of my Guiding career because I had to be everywhere where Lady Baden-Powell was while she was in Ely. I had to carry her mac, show her where the toilets were, all sorts of very mundane things but I felt very important and I'll never ever forget that day because there were so many Guides, Brownies, Rangers, there were all kinds of Guides at that particular service and it was quite a historic event.

Now also during my childhood I belonged to the St John's Ambulance. This was also during the war again and we were allowed, or asked to be, casualties when they had practices for air-raid casualties. Guides and St John's Ambulance and even the Red Cross cadets, we were all employed, free, we got no money, of course, but we did get pasted over with something, red dye, when we were supposed to be bleeding and we had our legs tied up with splints and things like that. And so we took part as very young children really, teenagers, in the war effort.

And in Littleport we had an annexe to the RAF Hospital which had been built in Ely, at the Grange, a very large house in Littleport which was the Transport and General Workers' Union place when the war wasn't on, we had the overflow and I can remember every Christmas during the war some of the organisations, either the Red Cross, St John's or the Guides, we sang carols to the forces. We went right through all the wards singing carols to the patients who then, of course, were in hospital blue. So we did feel that although perhaps our childhood was rather different, because it was all during the war, we did really feel we were part of the country. Looking at Dad's Army and things like that we say, "well, yes, we remember that sort of thing" and so were part of the war effort.

Well, now, going on to sort of the pleasures as well. School was a pleasure to me, we had the muffin man we used to see, he used to come along with his muffins on a board on his head. He used to come down Crown Lane and he would stand outside school and if we'd got a penny, well, he had a muffin, but they're not like the muffins we get nowadays, they were more bready, dough-buns in those days. And then the goldfish man would come, or woman, whichever it happened to be. And if you had a bag of rags you could get a goldfish, and I remember we used to go back after dinner with our bag of rags, then go home from school at the end of the afternoon with a fish, and one of my fish lasted for years and years and years, and great works when it died. I was so upset about that. So we had little things like, that gave us great pleasure.

June Strawson - Ely High School 1944

They were just collecting rags really, and giving away these. Now when it got to summer time we had ice creams, home-made ice creams at a shop, [Mr Butcher] made them actually in his shop. He sold some in the shop, but he also had a man who would go round on a tricycle with a box-thing on the front, and he would sell his ice creams. Now they was really special ice creams. I expect it was really custard powder plus dried milk or something, but they were really good ice creams and they were so cold that it gave you a pain over your eyebrows and we always say "Oh, that's as cold as Butcher's ice cream", and it takes everybody in Littleport back to the 1930s. So that was something quite unusual, so we mustn't forget that, he used to be a photographer as well. Oh yes, he was a photographer, he did all sorts of things when you come to think about it. You could go and sit down on one side of his shop and eat your ice cream and I remember there were glass-topped tables and you had your ice cream in a little dish with a wafer and a spoon. And that was really heaven, because that was something your aunts took you out for. I had some lovely aunties and they used to take me for that sort of thing. My feet wouldn't reach the ground, I was so tiny, and I can remember that, my feet never reached the ground in Butcher's shop. But they sold postcards and all sorts of things, and talking of characters, because he was certainly a character, was Mr Butcher, and he had a wife too, who was very busy behind the counter.

Christine Kerswell

I remember the day the King died, I was, it was my first year at the High School. We were waiting for Miss Tilly to come and teach us RI. She was late, she was usually late, but she was very late this time. When she did arrive she told us she had been listening to the announcement on the radio and she told us the King had died. I remember everywhere else in England proclaimed the new Queen, but Ely didn't seem to consider it was

Christine Kerswell - Broad St Junior 1950

16

necessary. It wasn't until there was a lot of fuss and bother, that they decided they would issue the proclamation. It was later than anywhere else and consequently Gaumont British News, the newsreel cameras, came to see this place, proclaiming the Queen later than anybody else and I remember that we went from the High School across the Palace Green to hear the proclamation. I think it was outside the Cathedral. Afterwards of course we went to the Rex cinema to see the proclamation in the news. Later when it was the Coronation we went from the school in a party to see the film "The Queen is Crowned". Because, of course, it was marvellous to see it in colour. On television it was in black and white. I remember I went to a neighbour's to watch it on television because we hadn't got a television then.

Maureen Scott

My mother was a marvellous woman when I was young she worked on the land I can see her and her friends now wearing the old fashioned type bonnets. As I got older she worked for Hope Brothers where she remained for many, many years. I had a pet jackdaw for years, Jack was extremely tame and everywhere I went Jack went too. When I first got him, my father had picked him up on the side of the road, he was so young he did not have any feathers. He had his own house and he could come and go as he pleased but we did shut him in at night. I had a black and tan dachshund whose favourite hobby was going into the garden and helping himself to the raspberries and blackberries. He could hear the ice cream cart a mile away and waited by the gate for his ice cream and cornet, if he didn't get one he would either sulk or throw a tantrum. I then had a green Amazon parrot, she was perfection, and eventually died from asthma. These were followed by cats and dogs. I then decided parting was too

painful so these days I love my son's animals after the grandchildren of course.

Lilian Martin

The chapel at West Row, the Baptist Church, played a very important part in our lives. My father was secretary there for about forty years and he was also a Sunday school teacher and of course I was in the Sunday school and my brother was too. My grandfather had been superintendent for some time until he died in 1953. Sunday was always a big day. We started off, my father went to feed his father's chickens and we'd go with him to help or hinder. We'd then feed our own chickens and then dad would be at the chapel to get things ready - hymn numbers up, water out and do all the various jobs that needed to be done. My uncle was the one who lit the old tortoise stoves and kept the place beautifully warm. Sunday service was at 10.45 and after that we had a cold dinner, the meat left from Saturday's joint, cold Yorkshire pudding, beetroot but hot mashed potatoes and a nice hot apple pie. Sunday school was at 2.30 and after that we'd all go for a walk and then come home to a beautiful tea. Sunday tea was the highlight of the week, a lovely white damask cloth on the table and fruit cake, jelly with fruit, salmon sandwiches and we'd have an enormous tea then evening service at 6.30 and after that an enormous supper to (which) we brought all sorts of people and then we'd have a sing round the piano. Sometimes it was RAF boys, sometimes Americans. Occasionally a German came, a Captain Werner Wilke. I don't know how we picked up all these people but we seemed to acquire lots of people who liked to have supper!

I remember back in 1942, when the cottage next door to ours, which belonged to my father, became empty, and Queenie and Ralph Reeve moved in there. They were newly married and they improved the cottage, I expect at their own expense. They installed water with a stone sink, and they restored the ceilings by putting plasterboard in between the beams, stripping the beams and blackening them, so it looked very attractive in their cottage, unlike ours which had whitewash over everything. They'd put a nice bucket toilet in the corner of their newly built shed. They even had a telephone, which had a receiver that lifted off and went to one ear, very interesting. I remember going gleaning with her which is something that I don't think is done now. They had a dog and she thought I was lovely because I was fairly attractive, fairly chatty, had lots of fair curly hair, and she always wanted a daughter like me, so she said. We were very good friends, and I'm still very friendly with Aunt Queenie, although her husband is dead. They moved out in 1947 and my mother's parents retired from London and they came to live there, and so that was another new era. I can remember in 1942 taking dockey to my father at where he worked and I'd go on my own, which was a three year-old. I remember being bridesmaid at my uncle's wedding in Bristol in August '42. I was three and a bit and wore a white satin dress sprigged with pink rosebuds and a poke bonnet and carried a basket of roses. There were two other [grown-up] bridesmaids, and then there was another little, bridesmaid with me and she also was dressed like me and carried a basket. In her basket was a yellow rose, unlike mine which hadn't got a yellow rose, and I wanted a yellow rose in my basket. So when we went to the reception we had to put our baskets on a ledge and afterwards I picked up the other girl's basket because it had a yellow rose in it, but I was immediately swooped on by, I think, the girl's grandma who said "Oh, my dear, I think you've got the wrong basket". Do you know, at the age of three

I felt hatred for that woman who'd taken my yellow rose from me. And so I decided when I got married I would have yellow roses and to this day I love yellow roses.

I also remember that we reared cockerels in our back garden and I can remember my father killing them and drawing them and plucking them. Mum would wrap them well in greaseproof paper and then brown paper and pack them up well and we'd send them through the post to London. I found letters recently to say that the cockerel arrived safely the next day and it was beautiful, it cooked well. Now you couldn't do that now, could you, send a chicken or a fresh cockerel through the post and guarantee that it would arrive the next day.

Something different. In 1943 my brother was born. I didn't know that he was due to arrive. The name chosen for him before his birth was David. He arrived on St David's Day, March 1st, 1943. Also [in 1943], my parents moved to a larger house where the workshop was. I remember this happening, and also my mother's parents moving from London in 1947, as they'd got some money, and so they decided we'd have water in our house as well. We hadn't got the money to put it in, but we took the water from their house, which had been installed earlier, and the pipe came through into our house and instead of getting water out of the well we now had running water in the house. We had a bath but no hot water. We boiled the water for baths once a week in saucepans and kettles. There sometimes used to be pieces of cabbage floating in the bath!

Leisure

Lilian Martin

Saturday was a special day. We used to listen to *In Town Tonight* and then we'd go to the fish shop with my friends. Even if it was dark we were allowed to go on our own and it was nearly a mile to the fish shop. We'd buy fish or chips, not both, the fish was sixpence a piece and chips were threepence. Usually it was just chips and we could eat them in the place on a scrubbed table or bring them home in newspaper and then we'd listen to what I think was Music Hall but I can't remember. Anyway it always seemed silly to me but it was part of Saturday and then we'd have our bath in a tin bath in front of the fire and then go to bed. I belonged to Girls' Brigade and there was also a Boys' Brigade. We had Christmas treats, a Sunday school outing, it was really lovely. My mother would take us to Ely about three times a year. Now my husband lived at Soham and could see the Cathedral from where he lived every day and so he never went into the Cathedral until he was 45 because he knew he could do it any time he wanted so he never did, but three times a year we'd come on an outing through the fens to Ely and my mother would allow us to climb to the top of the Cathedral and we'd also wave to the soldiers as we passed the RAF Hospital - that was quite a highlight. One February half-term when she took us she allowed me to buy a dozen baby chicks, I think they were cockerels, so that we could fatten them for the next Christmas. But I had some money left and at the end of the day I went back and bought two dozen more, they were little brown chicks, so I went home with three dozen baby chicks. It was cold weather and so we had to have them in front of the fire, in the living room, in a coop and I think several were casualties but we did fatten several up for Christmas next year. We also went to Bury quite a lot and I can remember our bus having to stop on a very weak bridge at Lackford while a convoy of army lorries passed over it and someone mentioned that the bridge would collapse and this terrified me rather.

Christine Kerswell

I remember my first trip to Hunstanton. Obviously, during the war years the seaside was out but after the war they cleared part of the beach, near the pier at Hunstanton, and we had relatives at March, who worked on the railway and they, the people from the railway at March, had an excursion train which went from March to Hunstanton and obviously we went on it. It was great fun, we went of course to the station at Hunstanton, right beside the sea. We got there, and we all trooped onto the beach, this section of beach, which was cramped, packed full. We had a lovely day, the sun shone, and I remember I went straight into the sea , no fear, and I had a black and red woolly striped costume that had belonged to my

Waterloo Celebration

mum's sister and obviously when the water got into it, it went big and baggy and I didn't care. I was really, really sunburned and peeling after the whole day on the beach, but it was a lovely day.

I remember when my father came home from the war, my aunt had been to Butlin's Holiday Camp at Skegness and told my mother what a wonderful time they had and she wanted to go there. So dad said that it was alright, he didn't mind. We went but he hated it because having been in the army he didn't like being regimented at all. We didn't go again but we always went to Hastings for our holidays because my dad had a cousin who lived on the West Hill just below the Castle and I remember Hastings was a wonderful place to go. We went on the train and that was part of the holiday because we went on a steam train from Ely to London and then the last part from Victoria to Hastings was by electric train. We thought that was wonderful because it was so clean but nowadays of course, steam is no more.

Another thing I remember in Ely, visiting my great uncle's shoe shop which was near the Cathedral in Minster Place. My great uncle's name was Charlie Pryor and I remember the smell of leather and watching him actually make shoes for people who had bad feet; he would line them with wool to make them nice and soft and I remember his shop was where the Scotch Wool Shop is now and I remember that next door there was a garage. You went through an archway and I think it was Price's Garage you could go to.

Ann Powell

We played simple card games, draughts, dominoes on the chenille tablecloth. Grandfather would never light the lamps until it was dark - oil lamps. My youngest uncle, who was to die in the mud and

slime beside the infamous Burma railway, had a trick when he would spit at the oil lamp chimney and make it sizzle for my entertainment. He cracked it once. For some reason they used to hang an open hairpin on the glass chimney. Perhaps this was to do with the glass expanding. Granddad would only have the wireless on for the news to save the accumulators. These had to be recharged and not wasted on Henry Hall and ITMA.

Initially, social life revolved around the church, Sunday school, youth fellowship and old time dances at the Railway Social Club, a converted Nissen hut but with a painted floor It sweated as the heat built up and the french chalk turned to a sticky gunge as we tipsy two-stepped and square-tangoed. A prized invitation was to the King's School Christmas dance usually reserved for High School sixth formers, but I managed to go when I was only a lower fourth. I had a blue taffeta dress, with a circular skirt and a mandarin collar. A proper youth club was started around 1950, in the buildings where the Jehovah Witnesses in Cambridge Road are now; the St Mary's parish hall was there too, used by the St John's Ambulance. In my time I was a Brownie with Miss Cross in the hut on the far side of Paradise. A King's Messenger with Miss Willink in the St Mary's parish hall and we made little cotton shirts for babies in India at a place called Wilocra where they had been missionaries. It rather amuses me in retrospect to think that while we were making little cotton shirts sent out to India, Ghandi was trying to persuade them not to send cotton in the first place. Miss Willink ran the afternoon Sunday school at the Central Hall in Market Street. She and her sister lived in the cottage at the corner of the Palace Green. They wore vast skirts knitted on circular needles and sensible shoes. We were sometimes invited to afternoon tea: minute sandwiches, pale Indian tea from a silver samovar.

I did some basic first aid with the St John's Ambulance and stayed long enough to learn to do envelope corners and put an arm in a sling. I also belonged to the Girls' Friendly Society. This met at the Trinity parish room run by Miss Street and Miss Redit. They took us on holiday to Herne Bay, Towyn, and Abedovey and Shanklin on the Isle of Wight. I saw the fleet anchored at Portsmouth for the first time. The swimming club took care of the summer months from the first icy dip - no heated water then - in May to mid-September I practically lived in the water. There was no daily training session for budding competitors , either, you could do it or you couldn't at competition level. I could and eventually swept the board. Inter-club matches with Granta were always disappointing. Granta was the swimming club at Cambridge and they could swim all winter in the University indoor pool - we had to start from scratch each year. Some of us competed at county level but not successfully. We did, however, have a champion diver Sonny Hale, and the men's water polo usually did fairly well. The highlight of the year was the swim through Ely when the water was unpolluted, the men and boys started from Newmarket Bridge and the women and girls from the old bathing place halfway between Newmarket Bridge and the High bridge, finishing at Appleyard and Lincoln's boathouse landing on the Annesdale Quay. In the evening we had races across the river and played water polo. Even though the river was unpolluted it did have in it the dark black fen soil hanging like powder and when you came out of the river you looked as though you were a chimney sweep.

But the youth club was the most enjoyable. The youth leader, a sports master at the King's School, was an ex Royal Marine, Mr Russell. There was snooker, table tennis, dancing, and competitions with other youth clubs. I managed to win a cup for public speaking on campanology. We went camping near Hemingford Grey and Hartford, a bit like scouts without the badges, but our days were numbered - all the boys went on the National Service and disappeared for two years. There were still the Saturday dances with Ted Day but once everybody had started courting it was not quite the same. Just after the war the Ely Amateur Dramatic and operatic performances started up again in the old Rex cinema; my father took me to see their productions, and gave me a lifelong love of popular theatre and opera. 'Quiet Weekend' was one of the plays; 'The Gondoliers', an operetta, 'Pinafore', 'The Lilac Domino'. Once I left school and went to work on the railway I could get to London and the West End for next to nothing. I was too late for the big American musicals like 'Oklahoma' but they soon followed on film. There were the big bands - Billy Cotton, Alma Cogan and Mel Torme, and a rare scramble to catch the last train home. This was just before Bill Haley and his Comets took off and Tommy Steel and Adam Faith and skiffle groups and the Rock Island Line. It was when young people began to be teenagers and not just slightly ungrown up grown-ups.

M. Scott - Glad and Brenda

21

Lilian Martin

May 1st in West Row was the day that the young girls went May-dolling. We looked forward to this - it never seemed to rain to spoil our fun. We would dress our dolls in their best clothes and arrange them round our mother's wicker clothes basket (the same one I slept in as a baby), then we would decorate the basket with blossoms - apply, quince and japonica - and posies of primroses and grape-hyacinths. The basket would then be covered by a sheet and we would go to the neighbours and friends to ask if they'd like to see the [May] dolls. A coin would be handed over and the basket uncovered for the person to see the dolls in the basket - most people would ask the dolls' names and which of us they belonged to. I expect we shared any money that was given!

Margaret Springer

My holidays, well Easter, was spent spring cleaning, and in the summer holidays I can only remember going away on holiday three times. Twice with a lady I call my grandmother, but she wasn't, to Sheringham and once to a Methodist holiday camp. But summer holidays were really good because I used to go cycling with a friend, we used to go as far as Bedford and St Neots. We cycled all over the place, most enjoyable, and the other thing I had to do in the summer holidays were gleaning, because we had hens, and had to go after they had gathered the corn. We used to eat well really, my mother always put eggs in isinglass for when the hens didn't lay and she salted runner beans. My father was a good gardener so there were lots of vegetables, and we also had a relative who was a butcher, so we had no problem about the meat so really I wasn't affected by the war, food-wise. The other thing my mother did was she bottled all the fruit we had from the garden, and also tomatoes so we were really quite well fed.

Mary Blyth

All right, yes, yes, skating. One of the things at Earith which is just down the road from Bluntisham is that there is the fen that floods every year, and this year it's been used a lot because it's frozen a lot of the time. Yes, and we noticed this year that they had some championships just after Christmas, between Christmas and New Year. It was flooded and it's obviously used by some skating club or association or something, and they obviously get in touch with each other very quickly because within a short while there are a lot of people skating on the fen, a lot of cars, and a proper car park is established, that people have to pay to go into. I think that's called Bury Fen - flooded deliberately - yes, Bury Fen.

Terry Staines

When I was a boy my main hobby was trainspotting, and the big day was the day when we cycled to Huntingdon. Four of my friends had very reasonable bikes, well made bikes, Raleighs and things like that with gears, and I had one which had been made for me, had ASP written on the frame, to make it look as if it was something like a BSA and in fact it was all spare parts which was exactly what it was made from.

Trainspotting eventually went and sport took over and then, of course, Father Time took over and I had to give up some sport, so for my hobbies then, I started stone polishing and we used to go round all sorts of beaches picking up stones and I would polish them and turn them into jewellery etc.

Then string pictures, as a family we started to make those as well, also while I was picking up stone, I would be picking up shells and I would make those into jewel boxes or any other kind of box that you would require. Stamp collecting, I worked for the Post Office in fact, my job was a kind of wholesaler. I would receive stamps for the entire area, and being the first person to open them and see them I got interested and I started saving them in '67 and continued until I left the Post Office in 1995, luckily able to get hold of all the faulty ones and the errors. Stamp collecting inevitably led to collecting of postcards, mainly postal type, and from there I went on the historical postcards, and I have a collection of several hundred at home. We also, to keep the children amused on trips, started to take down pub names and the children long-since stopped doing that, so I continue that. I also make models, aircraft etc etc and one of my favourite hobbies is to collect from car boot sales and from wherever else I can find them, the old 78s. I still have a wind-up gramophone which I play, when I do evenings for the ex-service association or for the older senior citizens in the village. They still like to hear some of these. And now that I've retired, last week I took delivery of a wood turner's lathe and I am now hoping to take a course and start to do that.

My main activity outside work has always been sport and most of my friends come from that particular area. When I was 12 I was invited to play for Cambridge Telephones in a national table tennis tournament - British Telecom it's now called but in those days it was simply a Post Office tournament and I was invited to play with two chaps, Tommy Catlin and Norman Harper-Scott. I left Ely at 4am and got home just after midnight and that was probably the most gruelling day of my sporting life.

I played table tennis for Ely, along with Margaret Garwood, as she was then known, Tony Evans, Geoff Brown, Russell Lane and Malcolm Fletcher. In those days there were not a great deal of cars

available to us and I can recall one particular instance where I biked to Black Horse Drove to play table tennis. I left about three quarters of an hour before the other two, who were going on a motor bike. When we finished the game it was getting towards evening and it was dark so Russell Lane was on his motor bike, his pillion passenger was Malcolm Fletcher. We finished up coming home from Black Horse Drove with Malcolm hanging on to Russell's waist and me with my arms round Malcolm's shoulders being pulled along on a bike all the way back to Ely.

John Martin

I will tell you about some of the activities that we did beyond the home. I was still young then. As a youngster there were plenty of other boys at home to play and we played such games as hide and seek, cowboys and Indians, top and whip, bowling the hoops, squares which you chalked on the pavement, played with kicking a stone, around and scored all sorts of points. We played with caterpillars, we made bows and arrows. Near our home there were some willow trees, and that was lovely because you could make bows and arrows from the willows which was very good. We played marbles and we went bird nesting, and there was always the recreation ground in Soham and there is still one there, not far from the Parish church, and you could go there and there were games to play, also all kinds of things - swings, slides, and so we always had something to play, never bored as children and sometimes we got into mischief - boys will be boys, and we got into mischief as well.

I remember one particular time that I shall never forget. My friend Charlie and I were hoping to get some rubbish for the bonfire we wanted to get ready for November 5th Guy Faulkes' day. We couldn't find any rubbish anywhere.

Charlie came along with his dad's barrow and axe and hook to cut the hedge with. I said, "What are we going to do?" He said, "We can't find anything, we will cut this hedge" which belonged to a nearby farmer. "Will he mind?" "No, he wants the hedge cut". So there we were cutting the hedge. Charlie had a go with the axe and I should think he got a bit tired, he said, "You have a go". Of course, no sooner had I got the axe than the farmer came along with his horse and cart, "What are you boys doing?" John threw down the axe and ran off home. When I got home to my sister, she said, "You're home! It's not dinner time yet". I said, "I know, I've got a headache, I want to go to bed". That was always the excuse. My family knew when I was in mischief because I'd always got a headache and want to go to bed, then so to bed I went. I remember that after dinner time Charlie came and knocked on the door, "Is John coming out to play?" and my sister said, "No, he has a headache, he's gone to bed". I shall never forget that. That is quite amusing looking back.

After about the age of 12 we could earn some pocket money - we could do odd jobs cleaning mangels and if you don't know what mangels are they are similar to turnips [or swedes] and were used for cattle food. Singling the sugar beet which is as the sugar beet was planted out and the plants are thick they had to be thinned out. Finally, you left a single beet about 8" apart. One could either crawl between the rows which was very tiring, crawling up and down the land, or you could bend down and do it that way. It was a painful job whichever way you did it, but at the end of about three hours you probably got 6d, which is 2 - 1/2p in today's money. Sometimes I could lead a horse - that was another interesting thing. A hoe would be towed by a horse, horse hoe we used to call it. There would be a man behind to guide the hoe, and the boy would lead the horse. Now mostly they were shire horses and those horses weighed about 1 ton and they'd have great big feet and the fellow who was guiding the hoe would say "Don't let that horse kick the beet". I don't know how you'd gotta stop this horse from kicking the beet as they had such big feet, and if he swung his head, one went with it. I never solved that one yet - how to stop the horse from kicking the beet.

With a bit of pocket money we could visit the cinema in Soham, there were about two at that time. I must tell you about one. One was an old cinema and often broke down in the middle of the shows and suddenly the film would stop and they'd be shouting, banging, until they mended the film and started the film again, and I remember people telling me that on one occasion when the film had stopped there was a rat that ran across the base of the screen and as this rat ran across the girls were screaming and the boys were shouting and someone shouted out "Bring a stick to kill the rat", and after that it was known as 'the rat pit' and then the war began. They built a new cinema, so that was nice go to the new cinema but still "the rat pit" was going and there was a bit of competition, I think. You could get a seat for 2d - I'm talking about old pence - or if you'd got a lot of money for 4d and be really rich and get a good seat.

M. Scott

School

Christine Kerswell

I started at Market Street mixed infant school in September 1945. It was only just up the street from where we lived and I hadn't far to go and I had been wanting to go for ages - watching other children. Mother took me on the first day and I remember I didn't want her to come and I told her to go away quite quickly. My first teacher was a lady called Mrs McClements, the Headmistress was Miss Hazel, there were also teachers Miss Knights, Miss Winchester and Miss Austin were teachers there. My second teacher was Miss Knights and my last teacher was Miss Hazel. We sat in double desks with seats that tipped up and were made of wood and cast iron. When we went into the playground it seemed huge to me but later when I saw it, it was very tiny. There wasn't a bell to signal the end of playtime, Miss Hazel would appear in the doorway and bang on the door with a big stick and we all got into lines and went into class. We had no toys to play with, we did write on paper and I remember that we had to use the covers of our books because

paper was scarce. We did PT in the playground in lines with coloured bands and that sort of thing.

Milk was available at 1d a day. I hated milk but my mother wanted me to have it. She paid for it so I had to drink it. I loathed it especially as we had open fires and in the winter they stood the 1/3 pt bottles around the fireguard to warm and it was even worse, it had skin on it and was revolting. We also had to have cod liver oil and orange juice each day and I remember we had to get into a line and line up and the teacher would give each of us a spoonful of cod liver oil and then went to the end of the line and when we got to the beginning of the line again we got a spoonful of orange juice - when I think about it now, how revolting because we all used the same spoon but nobody seemed to suffer. I left there in July 1947. I went to Broad Street junior girl's school in September 1947. I remember on the first day we went to our old school at Market Street and then we were walked down in a crocodile from Market Street to Broad Street school. The head there was Miss Archer and my first teacher was a

Soham Boys Council School

lady called Miss Plumb, she got married during my year with her and she became Mrs Chapman. I remember going to see her married I think at the Countess of Huntingdon church. When I first went to Broad Street school the girls stayed there for just two years and then for the last two years of junior school they went up to Silver Street where they shared part of Silver Street secondary modern girls' school. However during my time there a prefab was built in the school garden so my last two years were spent at Broad Street school. I walked to school, it wasn't too far from Market Street but when we moved to St John's Road I had about a mile to walk, there were no school dinners so I had the repeat journey twice a day. We used to go down Silver Street and through the park, I used to like that because we played in the park. When the weather was fine we'd go home through the cinder path at the back of Tower hospital and across Millpits to get home. There was nowhere at Broad Street indoors to do PE so all PE and games had to be in the playground and we had little mats we had to lie on and I remember

they were ridged and really hurt your back. I didn't like it at all.

We wrote in ink, it was powdered ink diluted and sometimes it was diluted so much you could hardly see it, it was very pale and we had homework and everything was geared to the Eleven Plus. Mrs Aley was the scholarship teacher as she was called. She used to really push hard to get as many through as she could. The Eleven Plus I remember was in three parts and the year that my class took it, fourteen of the class went straight through, passed the first - passed right through which was quite an achievement. The toilets there were horrible they were outside and they were smelly. I didn't go and I used to pretend to go and I didn't go because I hated it. Most of the girls came from Ely but we had two girls from Wentworth, they came in the last year because I think it was considered they stood a better chance of passing the Eleven Plus if they came to Ely school which they did; they both passed. But we also had some girls from the Chantry on the Palace Green which was a children's home and you could

The River - Soham

always pick the Chantry girls out, because they all had their hair styled in the same way, obviously the same person did their hair every morning.

We had homework every night and this increased as we got older. The uniform was a navy blue gym tunic, white blouse and a navy and yellow striped tie, navy blue beret, we always had to wear the beret or we were supposed to. In the sixth form we were allowed to wear a navy skirt with a white blouse. If you were a prefect you wore a yellow sash and a yellow beret. We wore gingham dresses in the summer and these were green, blue or yellow and we had to wear white or grey socks. Stockings were not allowed. I didn't like maths, I liked English and liked History. The history teacher was Mrs Staniforth and English was taught by Miss Defew and Miss Brooks. During my last year at the High School we moved to the new premises on Downham Road. It was quite an upheaval when we moved there, but I remember something called "operation shopping bag" in that vans came for the furniture and the big equipment, but every girl was asked to bring a shopping bag to school and we spent two or three days loaded with books walking up and down Downham Road, taking books from the old school to the new school. Quite a cheap way of getting them there and using manpower - or girlpower if you like. I remember the new school was opened by the Duchess of Gloucester and I can remember the garden flourishing the day before, instant roses and all sorts of things were planted and they were taken away again the day after the opening! On the opening the girls were all given the day off because there wasn't room for them at the school because there were too many dignitaries, but the prefects served tea and therefore I did get a look in because I was a prefect by then. There was no corporal

punishment but we were given conduct marks, they weren't for good conduct but were for bad conduct and if you got three or more you had to go to the head and have some sort of punishment. If you got a conduct mark of any kind you had to do something and I remember I had to learn the King James Preface from the Bible and there was a tally of the classes and of the forms and if your form got too many conduct marks it was not good at all.

Terry Staines
Having passed my Eleven Plus at the Silver Street secondary school I was given the [privilege] of going to the King's School Ely or Soham. My parents were very keen on me going to the King's School but I most certainly wasn't; all my friends were going to Soham, so I opted to go to the Soham Grammar School. It's a seven mile journey, it was undertaken by bus. Each day I would be picked up at Barton Square and dropped back there. The Head at the time was Mr Armitage, the other main teachers in my life were Mr Thomas who taught geography, Mr Hunt who did some science and gardening, Mr Waller who taught Latin. There was a mixture of day attenders and boarders. The headmaster had a house called the Moat and in there the boarders stayed and we would have fairly regular sporting fixtures against them. Uniforms were worn, they were compulsory. The uniform was a black blazer with red piping on the sleeves and all the way round and a typical schoolboy's hat, black with red piping on the bottom.

Sport was excellent at the school and we would be bussed once a week to the swimming pool at Newmarket and there we would be put through a series of lessons for some, tests for others the aim was to obtain a certificate of proficiency. I was a very capable swimmer long before I went to Soham and passed all of my particular proficiency tests on the very first morning and from then on was simply allowed to do as I wished in the pool. Cricket was one of the major sports, we had a very good teacher Mr Taylor who himself was a county cricketer, he seemed to take a shine to those boys who were good at sport, probably more so than those who weren't. He took a shine to me as far as cricket was concerned and I was often asked to stay behind and bowl against a member of the first team in the nets. This meant you missed the last bus home to Soham and you had a seven mile walk. Similarly, if you volunteered to go into various school and theatrical and dramatic productions - rehearsals would also involve missing the last bus and if one of the masters who lived in Ely was not in attendance then it was question of 'thumbing' a lift or walking all the way.

My reason for volunteering for dramatic and artistic things was simply to get out of Latin because the Latin master was the man in charge and you were excused your lessons for rehearsals which to me was a Godsend. Three times I walked the entire journey, once very deliberately just to see how long it would take, two by sheer bad luck I didn't get a lift, but mostly we got a lift just out of Soham, it wasn't really as bad as it seemed. The punishment of the day would be issued by school prefects or possibly masters and you would have to write out the 23rd psalm a certain number of times depending on the crime or you would have to write out so many times tables, again depending on the crime. For example, if you failed to wear your hat on the school bus that was worth three times the 23rd psalm. We had one young lad full of enterprise who did nothing with his spare time but write out the 23rd psalm and he would sell them to you at 3d a copy, and I think that man was deemed to be a big businessman!

My father died when I was twelve and this had quite an effect on my school work or appeared to and my class position deteriorated very sadly and I was hauled up with the other wrong-doers to the headmaster and I was actually stationed last in the queue and it wasn't particularly pleasant as everyone in front of me got six of the best on the backside. I could hear the yells and the screams from inside his room and I went to last and fortunately Mr Armitage was a sympathetic man who seems to believed that the entire fault of the world with me was because my father died and he therefore excused me and simply punished me in another manner. Failure to make it into one of the football or cricket teams meant that you had to do a cross-country run, we all dread those. You had to run out of the school ground over the railway crossing, over what is known as the horse fen at Soham up onto the Wicken Road, along to the railway bridge back into the horse fen and reverse the journey, and to make sure that people like me who detested cross country did our bit. Mr Thomas, a little Welshman, would bike along the road between the Wicken entry and the railway bridge and he would walk or ride behind us waving in front of him an old bicycle tyre which he has cut into two and if you happened to be in his way you got hit. He didn't like it but we simply jumped into the field beside the road where he couldn't reach us because we were out of his way.

Other various quirks, we had Mr Lawrence, who was our maths teacher, he would leave the main school building and walk across the playground. One of us had to stand beside our classroom door and he would call out a number between 1 and 12 and if in the 20 seconds that it took to get to us we hadn't written out that times table you certainly knew how to do it by the end of the day. We had a Mr Foster who had a favourite occupation, he

28

was a tank man in the war and had an old tank aerial onto which he tied a fishing line and at the end of that was a piece of chalk and he would click that across the class to the offending pupil. The history master would throw a tennis ball at you, not very painful, but Mr Riley the French master, a man for whom I had great respect, he would actually throw the board rubber at you, one half of that was wood and the other was compressed felt and it was just down to luck which one of those sides actually managed to make contact with you.

We had marvellous inter-school activities, we would play various sports against schools in Ely, Newmarket, Bury St Edmunds and Newport, Saffron Walden. Organised trips were just beginning in schools to some of the major events like Cup Finals or major things in London, unfortunately I unable to take up much of this option because as I said earlier, my father died when I was twelve so my mother was left with what was known in those days as the widow's pension of 10 shillings a week so we obviously couldn't do too much with that. I took my GCEs and qualified sufficiently to stay on but unfortunately financial demands were such that I had to leave school in 1955 and I left Soham Grammar to get a job.

Ann Powell

I went to the Market Street Infants' school in 1942. I was taken to school once on the first day and it was made quite clear to me that was the only time I was going to be taken to school. I must come home and go back on my own. I was taken along Broad Street, told where to cross, turn, cross Forehill onto the other side and up the hill round the Market Square. On no account was I ever to cross the Market Square. I must always walk all the way round the edge and I still walk all the way around the edge most of the time.

The first day at school we threaded coloured laces through a card. This was the classroom to the right in the recently converted building. This was the infant classroom, the one on the path. The school was L-shaped and there were four classrooms. One of them was divided by a curtain. These were the two senior classes. In the playground there were dustbins, heaps of coal and coke and the girls' and boys' lavatories, cloakrooms with pegs at infant height.

As I said, the first thing we did was to thread a coloured lace through a card. Round the wall of the infant classroom were cards with the alphabet and sample words. There was an old man on one of them and he was called "Old Hob". All the words only had three letters. Each morning we had prayers and learnt to chant the catechism. "What is your name M or N?" What on earth were M or N? "Who gave you this name?" "My godfathers and my godmothers in my baptism where in I was made a member of Christ, a child of God, inheritor of the Kingdom of Heaven". It wasn't explained to use, we just learned to chant it. Paper was short and the paper was torn into eight for sums and writing, and rubbed out time and time again until a hole appeared and then you could have a new piece.

There were no formal games only playtime and occasionally drill. It was wartime and there was a shelter through a gate at the bottom of the playground at the back of what was the Grange Maternity Home for evacuee mothers. When the siren sounded we all crowded down into the shelter and sat there with the expectant mothers. And I have often wondered what would have happened if one of them had gone into labour in front of all the infant school.

I moved from Market Street school in Ely to Broad Street school, which is where the computer shop has been opened now. It was the Conservative Club for a little while. It was girls only, there were two classrooms and it was ruled by Miss Rickwood who had a glass eye and a very bad temper.

We had a school band and I played the cymbals. We also made puppets from papier-mâché and acted out boring bible stories like Esau. Country dancing, but no formal games, only drill. There was still a bomb shelter in the playground for the buzz bombs or the doodlebug raids. I moved from there to Silver Street girls' school at 9. There were four classrooms and at 11 I was in Mrs Aley's class, the scholarship year. Unfortunately, she remembered my father poking fun at her husband's bowler hat when they were courting and she made my life a misery. But fortunately she did not mark the Eleven Plus paper and I passed and I was free of her. At these two schools, there were no uniforms, there were no school dinners, there were no formal games, only free milk. A few children who were very poor very badly dressed and one girl came in a ragged cotton dress and a threadbare jumper and wellingtons, summer and winter.

The headmistress of the Silver Street school was Miss Seymour and she had a thing about music and once a year we were drilled for choral service in the Cathedral with Miss Seymour waving her hand limply in the front. It was a complete mystery to me what she was doing. No one ever explained rhythm and tempo.

I went to High School in St Mary's Street, it had been a private school until the education Act of 1944. In my year there were 90 scholarship girls divided into three classes. A, Alpha and Remove. The lessons were formal, with dictation. The odd progressive teacher who invited discussion lost control of the classes. Punishment was lines, being kept in, there was no corporal punishment. Our uniform was navy blue gym slips, berets and macs with white blouses, ties, scarves knitted or the striped university felt type scarf.

We had to have plimsolls and house shoes, what on earth were house shoes, nobody ever said. There were no gangs there, just groups of friends, we were not allowed to eat in the street, and had to wear our hats at all times. There was no question of me going onto further education. I left school at 16 and went to work the next week. Further education did not come until they encouraged people in the 70s to do further education as mature students.

May Turner
This will have to be off the top of my head as I haven't made any notes. I was born in Suffolk in 1913 but on the death of my father, who worked at Ickworth Park Estate, my mother had to leave the tied cottage and come home to live with my grandmother and grandfather; my grandfather and grandmother brought me up. I should think at the age of four I went to the mixed infants' school in Clay Street and no doubt my mother took me for the first day, but after that I would have been in the car of my cousin who was six years older than I was and she would have been then attending the Junior School which was also in Clay Street. So she had to take me to the infants and then go onto her school and I think I must have been only a thorn in the flesh of my cousin who had to look after the other child and leave her own friends. To get home to dinner we walked, we went through the churchyard and down to Hall Street and back again after lunch and we also made a point of calling in the Post Office

because grandfather worked there and we could always get a sweet and a penny off grandfather if we had been good at school. After the infant school we would have gone into the juniors and by the way, the infant school must have been pre-war building (1914-1918 war), it was very commodious and had a very nice time there. Then juniors we would have been girls only and there was a beautiful kitchen arrangement so we were taught to cook and we did a lot of sewing too. Then we move into the higher school which was run by the church so the vicar who was the Reverend Rust and Mrs Rust paid us a lot of attention. He would come to give us religious teaching and Mrs Rust always judged the needlework class every year and I remember a Miss Hunt who was a local teacher, she was very food of country dancing and we always had to do country dancing for the vicar and his wife to keep the old things going. It was a very old building with no separate classrooms, just brilliant red curtains drawn across to separate us and you could always hear what was going on and you always knew when Miss Jelly the headmistress was

coming 'cause the bay would fall terribly quiet and you knew you had to got to be quiet when she ripped the curtains back again and pointed a some 'cause she had to pick on someone who was making a lot of noise and that was as much as I can remember.

John Martin

I'd like to say a little more about the second school I went to. In my life I only went to two schools, the first one was the Infant School and the Elementary School which we went to when we were seven 'til we were fourteen. As I've said before, that was nearer home and that was in walking distance and that's how we got to school. The building it was a very strong building there was a hall and six classrooms there and the teachers used to each every subject, so when you got there at the age of seven you went into standard one and when you was eight standard two, and so on and when you got to the top class you had Six A and Six B. First of all you went in Six B and then later in Six A. As my sister used to say, leaving school at fourteen that was a bit too early because

Martin - Maternal Grandads House

31

having spent a lot of time learning to read, learning to write, learning your maths, so when you got to fourteen that would be the time to start learning the lessons of life, but that was too late because one had to go out to work then, but as I said before, I enjoyed school.

The teachers were marvellous really, they had patience and they were firm with us, there was discipline, unlike some homes and some schools' lack of discipline, there was discipline, but they were kind. If you got into trouble you possibly had homework to do or sometimes stay in school when the others had gone home; the stay in school was called detention as the teacher used to explain you were detained for about half an hour, and you did sums or you did reading or something of that nature, that was a punishment which was not very severe but the fact that all the other boys had gone home and you were still there was punishment enough. I remember one English lesson we had I could never spell the word 'necessary' so the teacher said, "Tomorrow when the others have gone home you will write out fifty times the word 'necessary' ". NECESSARY. I've

never forgotten how to spell that word! If I write I shall always get the word correct - NECESSARY. It was a good way of learning; also the teacher would - this was in Form 6 of course when we were supposed to know these things - and whatever lesson was on he would suddenly dart out and say, "6 x 8" or "5 x 4" or "20 x 4", all that kind of thing so you really got to know the tables of course. I understand the children don't learn tables now, but we used to learn the maths tables up to twelve times table and now we can remember. In this age of computers we can say 5 x 10 = 50 and 4 x 8 = 32? Yes, I think I've got that right, that's good for the memory.

I left school in 1940 and after the war began we had some of the evacuees from London and they came from East London bringing some of the really rough boys and girls. Because ours being a boys' school there were some rough boys also. [However] the local boys could match them because they'd got their friends. The bit I'm proud of, the evacuees really because if the boys from London played up there were boys from Soham who would be able to deal with them and they'd got

M. Scott - Horse Plough

their mates there anyway. Sadly, the evacuee boys of course were outnumbered anyway, but we soon got friendly with them and even years after that some of those evacuees would come and visit the people they used to stay with because they really got to love the homes they were fostered in and I know my aunt had two evacuees and they used to come and see her quite often, even up to the sixties so that was really good, some good friends were made by them.

Other school as I said I left in 1940 when I was fourteen I tell my son now I left at thirteen. I say yes I did, at the end of the term was in July and my birthday was 2nd August so I was actually thirteen when I left school and I started work next day, so I started work at thirteen, one of my brothers [started work] at eleven, so that was something in those days. But I didn't leave home as such and you may have heard me say after father died when I was ten, the home was split up and we were all separated and I went to live with one of my brothers and sister-in-law in the nearby village of Barway so I didn't' actually leave home when I left school because Barway was then my home.

I forgot to mention a part of my childhood when I left the Soham area and lived at the village of Duxford for a time. It happened like this that my oldest sister [who] was working in Ely, had an offer of going as housekeeper to a man who was working on a farm at Duxford, and she agreed to go providing that I could go with her because she had brought me up from childhood, and was very attached to me, I suppose. I was like a little child to her although I was the younger brother. So off to Duxford I went. This was about 1937, and we lived actually near the aerodrome which was quite exciting at that time, not realising that the war would soon be upon us.

As much as I remember, the aircraft that were there were Tiger Moths because some of the lads were still training, they were flying, but they were still under training. I remember quite vividly that one day there were three that were flying together collided, and down came one of the planes and killed the pilot. This was quite traumatic to witness an aircrash. We always used to look up and see the planes flying but to witness a crash was something really outstanding.

Now, I went to the village school of Duxford which was Church of England school. I well remember one occasion when we used to cycle from the farm to the village to the school, and when I came out of the school the bicycle tyres were flat and I went round the back to the teacher and she said, "What's happened?". I said, "My tyres are flat, someone must have let the wind out of my tyres". "Well", she said, "find out who it is", she said, "and make them pump the bike up". And afterwards I thought well, strange lads, they'd all got their friends, probably two or three lads had let the wind out of the tyres and I was a bit timid in those days. How can I go and say "Well, pump my bike up". Anyway, I borrowed a pump and eventually got home. I remember that quite well. I thought silly teacher, fancy telling me to go and tell other boys to pump my bike up. That was not on. Later on, I went to the Sawston Village College, after being aged eleven which was really something, for the Village College was something really quite new in the Cambridgeshire area. A good thing, I remember, was that they had hot dinners which we hadn't been used to.

They were quite adventurous at Duxford on the farm because at harvest time I remember there were lots and lots of rabbits, the gamekeepers were there but the rabbits were there also, and we had rabbit pie, rabbit pie, rabbit pie, so much that we got tired of rabbit pie.

Anyway, we moved back again to Soham or Barway actually in 1938, just before my sister died, but that is another story for later on.

Lilian Martin

My first school was at West Row junior school - you started there 4 or 5 until 11. My brother was born in 1943, I was nearly four and wanted to go to school then. So my mother arranged for me to go as soon as I was four and she cycled down with me leaving the new baby with the next door neighbour, but of course I wanted to come home for lunch, it was nearly a mile away and it was difficult for my mother to fetch me so I had to stay to lunch. Lunches were 2 shillings and a penny [per week]. I enjoyed everything except bread and butter pudding which to this day makes me heave at the thought.

The school was originally built in the 1870s and I know that my grandfather was one of the first to attend there. A large hall had been added in the 1930s, meaning that we had a large assembly hall that was suitable for games and dancing. Country dancing which we had to do and it was alright as long as the boys that we had to dance with hadn't got dirty hands but they often did have and smelt a bit. The only thing that wasn't very good was bucket toilets in the playground, and they were grim places. At the beginning of the war an air raid shelter had been added and I remember going in there wearing a Mickey Mouse gas mask. I was first put in the beginners class with Mrs Alexander who was tall and attractive and very kind, but I soon learnt to read and do sums. I was promoted to Mrs Norman's class which I didn't enjoy at all. She was sharp and shouted and wasn't kind like my first teacher but I enjoyed school and wouldn't

stay away and arrived half to three quarters of an hour early.

The school didn't start until 9.30am because the fen children had to come in by bus and before that they had quite a long way to walk to get on the main road, so they had to start from home very early, so our school started late. At first I walked to school but later I cycled.

The lessons were the usual ones and we did needlework and we learned how to do embroidery as well as make clothes which I never learnt at my other school. We had plays at Christmas and I can remember being Fairy Light of Gold if you would believe it. I was always a head taller than anyone else but my final part was Angel Gabriel and I stood on a chair wearing someone's wedding dress. I had hair down to my waist and I felt that this was my crowning glory, this was as if I'd arrived! I'd played the principal part in the nativity play but I fell off the chair as I was getting off in my wedding dress.

As I finished the end of my first school I was ten years old. It was drummed into us that the Eleven Plus exam would soon be taking place, the headmaster gave extra lessons to a privileged few, i.e., the children who belonged to builders, farmers, or people who'd got money but of course my father was a farm labourer, we had no money and so I was excluded. We cycled to Mildenhall, which was three miles away to take the exam at the Secondary Modern school and then had to wait until April or May when I was surprised to see my mother come into the playground. She never came to the school and she didn't make that much fuss of any of our achievements but she came to the playground, and it was a lovely sunny day and the teachers were all in the playground standing in a group talking and she went up to them and handed them a letter and it was a letter to say I had passed the eleven Plus exam and as it happened I was the only one so they hadn't had much success or at least the headmaster hadn't been very successful with his extra tuition.

Anyway I started at Newmarket Grammar school in September 1950. It was a very small school, at the time I went there we had the most children they'd every had and that was about 200 boys and girls. It was housed in an old house and the classes took place in the living rooms and bedrooms and we could have a maximum of 30 in a room at a push, but as it happened there were so many [had qualified in 1950] that they had to build another classroom and so there were 22 in each of two classes because 44 had gained enough marks to go that time.

It was an hour's bus ride from my home and I was one of the first on the bus. The bus was a double decker and it had stood outside all night and when it was frosty it was very, very cold but we amused ourselves, we did our homework on the bus and got into trouble for having shaky writing. We had bus feasts, we played games, we even had a firework display. It's a wonder we are alive because we had sparklers, pretty matches and then someone had a small firework that shot out pretty colours but unfortunately the bus jerked and the firework rolled over and rolled along the aisle, still burning away. So it's a wonder the girls weren't all burnt to death but they survived.

Mr Watterson was the headmaster and he seemed very old, I though he must be in his nineties then but he died just six years ago aged 99 so he obviously wasn't as old as I thought.

There were no facilities at the school for games and art and so we walked to various parts of the town in Newmarket for art lessons, cookery, the games field was a long way away and I hated hockey. We went to the Drill Hall for PE which I didn't mind, and there were no changing facilities there so we played in our gym slips and I remember falling over on that floor one day at such an angle that all the splinters went into my behind and tore my gym slip to pieces, the back of it, so I had to lay on the floor and teacher pulled out hundreds of splinters from my behind and that night when I got home I took my gym slip to pieces because the back was ruined and I took the front off an old gym slip that had worn out - they had box pleats and the box pleats disintegrated eventually. So I took the front off one gym slip and the front of the one I had been wearing and sewed them together to make a new gym slip because mine wasn't fit to go to school in. I hated French and the master shouted, but loved biology, RE and music and used to come top usually in all of these three. I was good at English but not so good at geography and history and poor at physics. We had assembly every day and twice a week the physics master played a record, he played the Arrival of the Queen of Sheba and for years that became my favourite piece and I'm sure it was because of the music played in assembly that I came to appreciate good music. We had outings to various places - the Congregational Church where the head boy played the organ, we went for a tour of London when it was the Coronation. I can remember going to Oxford and Blenheim Palace, Hampton Court, Kew Gardens, etc.

Phyllis Trevers
Downham Feoffees Mixed. Everyone loved it. That was my top school with Mr and Mrs Crabbe. Mr Crabbe had married a Miss French who lived on Back Hill. You never knew her brother Clem? Clem he was a poor old chappie he used to go

down the station and meet all the men who were bringing their wares up to Ely town and he'd drop their bags and boxes at different shops. In the infant school we had those tin trays with sand and a slate. Yes, you know, like you make swiss roll with. Well it was a tin like that and you made a,b,c,d at my infant school. And we used to have little concerts as well, and at this concert I remember once we all dressed up in our nightdresses and had candles.

Yes, and I'll tell you. My mother borrowed a posh nightie from one of the girls in the village because mine were very ordinary (probably made out of an old sheet or something). We had these candles and we each sung a little bit. Then we lay down on the floor and went to sleep. And another thing we did, while we were there, we each took currants, sultanas, raisins, eggs, flour and we made plum puddings, Christmas puddings, at that school.

At the infant school my teachers were Mrs Foot and Miss Wells and then a pupil teacher, Lily Frost. (She's still in going gear at Little Thetford, so I think). And then at the top school I had Miss Pate, yes, and Mr & Mrs Crabbe. Mr Crabbe was headmaster. He's come back from the war and got a job. I can see the slate there and if you were very, very good you were allowed put how many children were at school that day. When we went and got the register, there were about 100 pupils, thirty children in a class. I was thirteen when I left but having my fourteenth birthday during the summer holidays. I didn't have to go back to school. I remember Miss Wells. She came from Dersingham and there were fir trees in her village and she brought back some nuts which the little squirrels had chewed and she also eventually had a squirrel stuffed for us and put in a cupboard and that was a great day you know, rather a possession having a squirrel put into a glass case. There was no Eleven Plus exam, only a class exam to see how well we had done.

Mrs Crabbe, my teacher, she wore glasses and I was a rare old talkative one (still

am). She said "Quiet, quiet, I want everybody to attend to the lesson". She sat at her desk you see and I went to say something to somebody. She said "Phyllis Yardy, stand up and go out. You're talking". She had seen my reflection in her glasses!

I remember Mrs Crabbe being ill once and we children all collected at one end of the top school Her bedroom window was in the school house just there and they opened her window (she had scarlet fever) and we sang her favourite hymn.

There was a very bad thing of scarlet fever at the time and one girl she died, and there were about five of us, I think. There's still five of us alive, and we went down to the chapel, the Wesleyan chapel down the other end of town, and we were allowed to march in front of the cortege and we sang "Safe in the arms of Jesus, safe on his gentle breast" and we were carrying a wreath, two of us. And this wreath was of artificial flowers with a globe over it and we went down to Little Downham cemetery to her graveside. I must have been, I suppose, about eight or nine.

I remember tortoise stoves in both schools. And you children who came from the fen up to our school, you had to walk about three miles and you got very wet sometimes and we hung all the clothes around the guard of the tortoise stove to dry them before they went home. If they had to go home over the railway they were always allowed out before "the fourer" went - the four o'clock train. Because my father told the time by the trains going through.

Edna Nunn
We didn't have either sand trays or slates but I do remember being in the Pymoor infants and having paper with two narrow lines and we had to copy from this blackboard, the letter it would be about my first day at school. Mrs Smith the teacher went into see my mother and said "Have you thought of having Edna's eyes tested?" and my mother said "No". The teacher said "Well, she's either completely stupid or she's short sighted". So from five I was taken to Mr Gardiner's to have my eyes tested and yes, I was very short sighted and I had these glasses and I was the only child at Pymoor school wearing glasses and I hated it because Mr Smith gave out, "Nobody is to borrow Edna Barker's glasses, nor to play with them". The children probably wouldn't have noticed if he hadn't said that. They were very useful. They were little horn rimmed, circular horn rimmed specs with gold bits and in scripture lesson I could catch the sun on the gold bits and dazzle the other girls.

Mary Blyth
When I was about six years old I was evacuated with my grandmother to an aunt and uncle who lived in a village near Peterborough. I remember they had quite a long bungalow and I think he had probably moved up to the area because of his work. I can't remember the name of the village and there's nobody now I can ask. I went to the village school which was a typical village school I should imagine. It was one room divided in the middle by a sort of half-wall with a gap in the middle. In between there was a big coal boiler which heated both the rooms. The younger children were at one end. The older children were at the other end of the room. There was only one teacher who moved between the two. By that age I could read and write and do sums quite well. I remember I was quite in advance of all the other children and I think because of that I wasn't can't remember feeling welcome in the school, and I just felt that I didn't belong at all there.

I was probably up there for about nine months and in the end my parents came up to visit me and I suppose they could see that I wasn't that happy and they weren't happy without me so they took me back home again. It was a private arrangement but there were the doodlebugs.

We were girls only right from the junior school. It was stupid because I do remember at the technical school [when] we were 16 years old it was quite a big event when the window cleaner came - it was a man on the premises!

I was a bit like Edna. I found it difficult to talk to boys but I was lucky in that I had begun to go to a Church Youth club so that I was coming into contact with boys. My first boyfriend was my husband when I was actually twenty-one but until then we had gone around in a mixed group, which was good. That was one of the best times of my life.

I remember in the junior school we did a lot of drama and it was never scripted.

We had an outline and I suppose it was a way of getting us to speak. This is where the spiral staircase came in because we always used to bring that in as much as we could because it was the only time we were allowed to use it. I don't remember anything at secondary modern school but when I went to Technical school, to the annexe, we had a lovely garden and we did an open-air production of 'Hiawatha' There were lots of fir trees and I was Nokomis, and then we went to the main school I remember one lunch hour there were a lot of girls and when it was wet we were in the Hall. The headmistress, who was a very stately lady, came in and said "That girl over there, you were in Hiawatha, weren't you?" and I said "Yes", she said "I'd like you to sing it now". She made everybody stop and I had to sing this thing unaccompanied much to my embarrassment. There wasn't much drama there but there was a very good school choir. I was in that and the teacher really stretched us, we'd do Britten's Ceremony of Carols, etc. I suppose my main interest in drama has always been as a watcher because once I

Cross Green - Soham

began to go to work in London and they had a scheme where you could book a seat on the day for 2/6d I went to the theatre a lot then for a good few years.

Maureen Scott
First of all I attended the Littleport school as my mother had done before me but where her hair was so long they tied it to a chair, mine was very short. I particularly remember one of the teachers, Miss Howard, when she was on playground duty we wound her up with a pretend key in her back and she walked about like a clockwork doll. In fact, she looked a bit like a clockwork doll - she had quite a plump round face, short black hair, and she just looked like a doll. I then went to Ely High school where I remained until I was sixteen. As June has already said I also remember the fishman along with the 'nit' nurse, the doctor, the dentist and the school inspectors. The junior school was a mixed one and you stayed in the same classroom, apart of course for assemblies and concerts, etc.

M. Scott - Record Player

M. Scott - Mums family

When I went to Ely High school you had a different classroom for every lesson and of course a different teacher for every lesson. This took some getting used to. One of the good things was the fact that your friends changed; instead of just friends from the village they now extended to the whole of the Isle of Ely. I had lots of good friends like Margaret from Ely and Jean from Sutton, etc and I used to stay with Margaret in Sutton and Phyllis in Haddenham, those were the days. I was twelve before I could swim, even then I was not very good, but every day in the season home on the bus, straight into the river, homework later. After they changed the course of the river we never swam again because it was too dirty. At school in Ely, we did quite a lot of walking, down near Ely station was the swimming pool, so in crocodile to the Paradise sports field for hockey and arts classes were in a room over the Club Hotel where the Mews is now.

I also made some good friends belonging to the central Foundation School from London, two girls from that school plus myself did a home-made concert for family and friends to raise money for the aid to Russia fund and I still have a letter of thanks from Clementine Churchill to prove it. Making friends - Kathleen and Pat who came from Finsbury gave me lots of outings and holidays in London. I felt quite privileged as we would visit the Finsbury Park Astoria a lot and I saw most of the stars of the day. Like Anne Shelton and all the bandleaders. These evenings at the theatre fascinated me as [the ceiling] was dark and twinkled with stars. Whilst at school I remember winning a prize for religious studies and when it came to Prize Day, which that year was held in the Rex cinema, I had to walk down the aisle almost from the back to receive my prize, I hated that walk and found it most embarrassing and have tired

to avoid that type of thing ever since.

Edna Nunn

Mr and Mrs Smith were very close friends of my parents. They made a great fuss of me as a tiny child. I can remember them coming in after church and playing with me and I watched Mr and Mrs Smith go to school standing at our gate. I waved to them. I loved them and I couldn't wait to be five to go to school. Nobody prepared me for the fact that when I got there it would be very different. I think what happened was that after a few days I got up out of my little desk and went to sit on Mrs Smith's lap and she tipped me off, hit me and told me to sit back in a very different voice that I ever heard used before. I screamed and I screamed and I can remember my mother dragging me to school the next day. My sister was also at that school and she was crying because there was this scene going on and the headmaster, Mr Smith, put me in the cloakroom and let all the children watch me scream until I went hysterical, and I felt awful, I'm sort of going goose-fleshed as I talk about it now. It stayed with me and affected my relationship with other people for years and years and years. The awful thing was, then it was obviously arranged that I would have a year off from school, then I would go back into Mrs Brown's class but auntie taught me during that time and I loved learning - I still do.

She was a lovely person, but you see auntie, as in your case, had got me ahead, lack of some understanding, they hadn't gone to the school and said how much does she need to learn, so I had done more sums than they had. The other kids hated me. I was bored and I hated it if they asked me to read because I knew I could read and the other children couldn't. All the time I felt different and Mr Smith was horrid. He was always dragging me out to the front to do things. It wasn't

40

until Mr McKee came that I was happy in that school but then I left when I was nine to go to Ely.

No one had realised how short sighted I was until I started school, I can remember I sat on the front bench. The benches in the infant school were long and they seated about four children on a bench - I was sitting on the front bench. Mrs Smith called in to see my mother and said "Either Edna's completely stupid or else she's short sighted because she can't copy anything from the board". I had my eyes tested and then I went to school in little tiny glasses. Again, I was made to feel different by Mr Smith but they had their uses in scripture, as I've said before.

When I was nine I took the scholarship exam and I passed and I was ten by the time that I started at Ely High school - problem of transport at Ely. We were about six miles from school, in the summer I cycled and in the winter it was dependent on someone taking me in a van or in a car (whoever was available) and that produced problems. I sympathised with Gwen Stevens who said you know that she longed for a train ride or a bus, because I would stand outside Ely High school waiting for someone to come and pick me up and I've known what it was to be the last one there on a winter's evening. Because I was so young - from Pymoor to Little Downham was open common in those days, and my sister who was six years older had just left her school - and every day she was sent to cycle with me to Little Downham where I picked up another girl to cycle with me and was sent to meet me in the afternoons. One particular afternoon we were playing about holding hands and pulling each other along and she pulled me off and I skidded along the gravelled edge of the road and gouged out me knee. I was taken into Guildacre farm by Mrs

Harrison who put the best that she had on which was cream. My sister rode me home on the back of her bike and my mother was horrified that she'd put cream on this ghastly knee. She was afraid of TB and she poured bottle of iodine on it, I can feel it now. The doctor said that it probably stopped TB but it meant that it couldn't be stitched up so I was in bed for five weeks.

I was working with children almost two years older than me and it was most stupid thing to do because I was way behind them all. All the way through until the fifth form I struggled and did nothing. I enjoyed my school days but I just didn't do anything. The headmistress when I first went was Dr Verini who was a delightful person. There were about three hundred girls, just over 300 girls when I started. The last two or three years Dr Tilly came and she was the headmistress. There was a teacher for each subject, in some cases two. Certainly for every subject there was a different teacher so there'd be quite a large staff, probably about 20. There was the headmistress, deputy headmistress, school secretary, maths mistress, biology mistress, geography mistress, history, art, games, cooking, the cookery mistress took us for sewing, French, Latin.

At Ely High school it was all girls. On very rare occasions if we had a very interesting speaker on a Tuesday afternoon the boys from the King's school were invited to come but we were shown in the hall first and we sat at the front and were instructed not to look round and there was this crowd of boys in their mortar boards came in and sat at the back. We were not allowed to look round.

June Strawson
I'm going to recall from 1929 onwards, not everything of course, but a quite resume

of what I can remember. To begin with, I must say that I went to school at four and a half and it was infants' school. Now in Littleport in those days we had three schools: the infants, the big girls and the big boys. Now that may seem strange to people from towns but from quite early times, it was a church school and from quiet early times the curate lived in a house in the middle of the big boys and the big girls school. The proper name, of course, was Littleport Town Girls' school and Littleport Town Boys' school, but were always, we always referred to them as the big boys and the big girls and we must explain this because when you got to seven, you left the infant school, you went up to the big girls and the big boys and you stayed there until you left school, from seven to fourteen. Now the only way that you managed not to stay there, although they were very good schools, the only way you managed to go away to school was if you passed the scholarship [to Ely High School for Girls or Soham Grammar School for Boys].

Now the Scholarship was a big word in capital letters, in the Littleport Girls' school, anyway, I don't know about the boys, but in the girls' school it was a really big thing, the Scholarship. And you had to sit an examination when you were ten, if they thought you would pass, and then if you didn't pass you could do it again at eleven, so you could have two goes at the scholarship and Miss Cheek was the headmistress. Now Miss Cheek was ably helped by another lady called Miss Howard, that everybody loved, we liked Miss Cheek but she was a very fierce but Miss Howard was very gentle and very different, and she taught in Littleport Girls' school right from when she left college to when she retired, so she had forty years straight at least at the girls' school, and she was quite a character, and she caught the train every day.

Now she caught the train from Downham Market to Littleport and she had, when I was at the school there anyway, a man used to take her up in his bus. Now he had a small bus, what would we call them

St Andrews Church - Soham

now, Oh minibus, but wasn't a minibus then, it was called Lofts' bus. Now Joe's bus often used to pick Miss Howard up from school, I suppose it was getting on for a mile from the school to the station, you see, and then she would catch the train home. Well, now, we loved Miss Howard and we almost used to fight to go down to the station with her, because in the summer days she would walk, she wouldn't have Joe's bus, she would walk if it was nice and we used to carry her bags and parcels and things back from the school to the station. Yes, she was a remarkable lady, and she taught grandchildren of her first pupils in the girls' school. I think she retired in 1940, one year after I went to High school. Miss Howard is not to be forgotten. Neither is Miss Cheek. She was different but she did a very good job there.

Now we used to get a holiday or half a day's holiday on Empire Day. Now we don't know about the Empire any more, or lots of people don't know about the Empire, but we had a holiday. And there was a gentleman in Littleport, I think he was probably a councillor, and I know later on he became a governor of Ely High School for Girls. Mr Peake was the man, and he used to come to the schools and we all met in the playground which was shared by the Infants and the Girls' schools and the flag was put up and we all stood around the flag and then he gave a little speech and then he declared the rest of the day a half-holiday.

Margaret Springer
My first school was Histon Junior School and I was there about quarter to nine, quite easily from my own every day. I enjoyed school but I don't remember much about it, came home for lunch and mainly I can remember it as a very pleasant experience.

I failed my Eleven Plus so therefore went to Impington Village College in 1947. I was rather worried about going to this school because you had to change classes after every lesson. I had to find my way around a rather large school and it took me at least a term to get used to this. I stayed to school dinners which I thoroughly enjoyed. I was absolutely useless at sport but I did learn to swim and was made to play rounders, hockey and netball. The only teacher I can remember was the art master and I couldn't draw and I kept asking form help and in the end, he decided I was a disruptive influence and had to go for extra maths which I was much happier at. During my stay at the school the 'O' levels came in and I think we had a year in which to prepare for them. I passed three, which wasn't very good.

Manners at school, basically, you had to stand up when the teacher came into the class. Apart from that I can't remember any other rules along those lines. At home you just didn't really eat other than when you sat at the table, and you certainly didn't eat in the street. Punishment, at home I was sent to bed if I did anything wrong or sent up to my bedroom and at school you had lines, standing outside the class, or sent to the headmaster. The history master was slightly different. If you did anything wrong then you had to learn a poem. I had to learn over several weeks, 'The Charge of the Life Brigade'. This was quite long but he was the only master who allowed discussion in his class. Otherwise you just sat there, you were taught and that was it.

■■■■■ Marriage and children

Peter Kerswell

I went to RAF Freckleton near Blackpool where I did training to be a medic. From Blackpool I went to the hospital at RAF Nocton Hall and from there I went to Ely in 1959. We were going to have a big St Valentine's Day dance but over half the medical staff had a severe bout of 'flu. Met my doom - Easter Monday 1959. Ted Day, who used to run the dances at the Corn Exchange, he said to me "What are you doing Monday?" I said "Not a lot". He said, "OK, come to mine. We'll have lunch then we'll go off to the races". We had a successful day - four winners out of five - first time I'd been to race course in my life. On the way back he said "What are you doing tonight?" I said I would go back to the camp. He said "Come round to mine, we'll have a spot of tea and then we'll go to the Corn Exchange dance". He said we had to go and pick up the band. He had a shooting brake. There was Dot Futter on the piano, Tom Langley on violin and Les Winter the drummer. Where the drummer lived was a cul-de-sac, not a well lit area. Out came the drummer with a lady. I sat in the corner because I knew they had to get in the back. Anyway, when we got there, much to my surprise, the young lady was not his wife but the daughter of the drummer. I can remember to this day what she wore - pink dress with a black velvet bow - I wonder how many other men can remember what their wives wore when they met them? We met on Easter Monday '59 and then in October '59 she went to college for two years. I used to go up and see her as often as I could in London and she came home in '61. She started teaching in Littleport. We just got settled down and then the next thing I was posted overseas for '62-'63 - I managed to miss the great freeze of '63 - do you remember that Phyllis? When it was all frozen. The river down by the Cutter...

I got married on 30th August, 1969. I'd known Chris for ten years but because of different happenings in life, it was 1969 before we got married. We got married in St Mary's church which is just across the way. Chris made her own wedding dress, it was white, Empire line. We had four bridesmaids, all her cousins. One cousin, Margaret, was still sewing her dress in the back of the car on the way to the wedding! Phyllis's husband Wilf took our wedding photographs. Our vicar was the Reverend Nobes who was curate. I always remember I walked down the footpath with my friend who was best man, Geoff Roberts, and when I opened the church door Felix Pilgrim, who was then verger, turned round and said "Who's the bridegroom?" I said "me!" "Six guineas please!" I thought, I'm not in the church, not married yet and he wanted my six guineas! Well, as I say, we got married and Phyllis's husband Wilf took the photographs. One of the bridesmaids, the youngest one, got stung on the arm - I always remember that. We had our reception at the Stage Coach Restaurant in Market Street which was then a very nice place run by Dennis and Edna Kancir, a very nice couple. Until they had that road accident we went there every year as near [to the date] as we could to our wedding anniversary. Edna always remembered. We went to London, Blackheath, for our honeymoon. All the family came to see us off on the line [train] from Ely - they all wanted to know where we were going to stay and we didn't tell them. The funny thing was we got on to the train and Chris said "Where are we staying?" I said "I've got the address" and do you know, I couldn't find it. Anyhow, Chris remembered it. We got to Maze Hill station and I went to find a taxi to go to the hotel. The next day I was in agony. I had - we had - had to walk up the hill and across the heath. I'd only got the one pair of shoes, I'd got blisters.

Lilian Martin

I got married in 1962 and came to Soham to live. I was shocked by the poverty in some areas of Soham. It seemed such a backward place compared with West Row and Mildenhall. There was - there were - elderly men in their seventies looking after disabled daughters, probably in their forties and fifties; there were people living in houses with dirt floors, with a sack on the floor, things that I'd never come across in West Row, which was fairly affluent because of the war and because of the aerodrome.

I'll just move on to our children, where they were born. I know people don't stay in hospital long now, but I went to the RAF [Hospital] to have the first one. Should have stayed in seven days but because they thought he had dislocated hips they kept me in for twelve days, so that he could see a specialist when the specialist came round. The next boy was born at the Grange, and again they measured his head because they thought he had hydrocephalus and I stayed in nine days then, three days before you were allowed out of bed and you had to use bedpans, which was awful! This was 1967. And then the third child, a daughter, was born at the Grange, no complications with her but I had a haemorrhage and was taken up to the RAF hospital in the middle of the night, for possible blood transfusions and the rest of it. Again, I was in there with her for nine days, and it was a lovely holiday, they waited on you hand and foot and eyebrow and fed you as well.

Perhaps I was unusual in that I stayed at home and looked after the children. My husband came home to lunch every day and the children, because they went to school close at hand, always came home until they were sixteen, and went to the sixth form at Ely. They came home and had my cooking every day until they were sixteen, so I imagine they're fed up with my lunches, which were not very imaginative. But after that I went to work in the library, which is next door to us now, and I enjoy ever minute of it.

We were talking about registering births, and my mother-in-law and her sister both found when they went to draw their pensions that they had been registered on the wrong day. We always celebrated mother-in-law's birthday on October 9th but she found in fact that she was born on October 12th and she said "That will do as long as they pay my pension". And then the next year her sister, who celebrated her birthday on October 22nd was told her birthday was actually October 24th. She said "Yes, that's fine as long as I get my pension".

Ann Powell

I had always want to go to sea and in 1955 I did the next best thing - I married a sailor. However, he was in the Fleet Air Arm and in 1957 he was posted to Lossiemouth in the north of Scotland, which was an airfield called HMS Fulmar. I followed him and lived in the bedsit - it was a contrast with the fens of course, but was very flat. We were at the seaside and we lived in the fishing community. Eventually, my children were born and I travelled backwards and forwards with them several times. I enjoyed leaving home, it gave a kind of freedom that was not found in a close-knit community. It was rather oppressive to young people at the time, the self-imposed rules were very strict, and what the neighbours thought, that was how they made people behave. The Navy was very much like the railway, once a part of it you were there for life and though I have re-married since, when I returned with my son it closes in around you just the same and you belong there.

Edna Nunn
My first husband and I met in 1956 and we married within six months. By that time my parents had died, otherwise I think they might have said something about it. My sister was concerned but I knew it was right but sadly he only lived for fifteen years. I had eight years on my own and I then married his brother-in-law.

My first wedding - my parents had died and my sister lived in Huntingdon so I stayed with her for a fortnight for residential reasons. We were married in All Saint's church on a Saturday on market day. No one had warned us of the market and we had to get through the market stalls. I wore deep blue velvet - I had this wonderful splash-out on my wedding dress. I went to Peter Jones in Sloane Square and they made my dress and a hat for me. I was determined I was going to wear an orchid and they flew an orchid up from Nice for me. My husband looked at

me as I came down the aisle and he told me after he thought "My goodness, have I got to afford to keep her!"

We went to the George Hotel in Huntingdon and they did the reception and Wilf, my second husband, was our best man.

Phyllis Trevers
When it came to Thursday and it was my half day I took my bus home to Little Downham. Sixpence return. I came back early, so I went to my friend Harry, who was Wilfred's brother, so after a while along to Bohemond Street came Wilfred. He said "I saw Phyllis". "Yes" they said "she's here waiting till 9 o'clock when she has to go back in". At about half past eight I said "Well, I'll have to go". Wilfred said "I'm coming a bit that way, I'll come with you". So he came, and we had a few minutes to spare so we sat on the Palace Green seat. I was quite fond of the boys and anyhow it had got to 9 o'clock so I said I had to go. Wilfred said "Shall I kiss you goodnight?" So I said "That's according to whether you want to". "Yes"

he said "I will". He said he would look for me on my half-day on Sunday. There were no buses on Sundays so he said he would walk with me half the way back to Little Downham, which he did.

That was the beginning of my courting. [I was] fourteen then. Well, it was friendship you see. Two brothers. Sunday came and he was hankering around Palace Green corner, there he was. "I told you I might come and walk half-way to Downham with you". "That's kind of you. Let's go". Away we went. We got to Mill Hill and along came my brother and sister to meet me. Well that was all right. Goodbye to Wilfred, he came back to Ely and I continued to Downham. Well, my mother was there as well and she said to my brother and sister "Not a word to dad about this". During the afternoon when we were having our tea, Joan, my sister, said "Wilfred Trevers tried to set his walking stick to see if he could make it grow". Mum looked across and dad looked round, so she said "Well, I might as well tell you, Harry's brother came to meet Phyllis and he's coming back tonight".

So he escorted me back home and so it continued - Thursdays and Sundays we were meeting. Fourteen, fifteen, sixteen, he was still coming. I was two years in that job. Then I left and I went to a house in Egremont Street - just taken over by the King's School. So he used to come to Egremont Street and meet me and walk me home. Thursdays I was all right, I walked round the corner and got a bus. Usually, Wilfred's brother was driving, so I was safe.

I became a cook at that house, I'd risen up from a skivvy maid and Mr Sedgewick, he was in charge of Hall's Brewery. There was another girl there and she also came from Little Downham so we were all right. We were given a room at the top of the house. I used to do the housework with a big hall with stones on it. I had to get on my hands and knees and polish that. That was all right, I didn't mind that. I became cook there and when I found I could cook fairly well, I got three pounds a month there.

I took a cook's job at Dr Beckett's in the High Street. I got three pounds a month there and my living-in. Still Wilfred was tottering about and that was ten years later. I was twenty-six when I married from the Beckett's.

[We] went back to Little Downham. Yes, it was the done thing. We had our house. My mum was a beautiful cook and she produced this, that and the other. Mrs Beckett came over to my wedding which was really very good for a mistress to come to a servant's wedding, but we were so happy in that house. Then do you remember Evans the taxi man? Well, he brought her over and when it was time for us to break up we were going to Maidstone for our honeymoon. Wilfred's brother was there. Frank, myself and Wilfred and Mrs Beckett all went back in Evans' taxi to Ely and we caught the train to Maidstone from Ely station.

It was a gold dress, the only long dress I ever had. I got it at Olive Coates in St Mary's Street. It was £3.50 - taffeta. She said, "You know, Phyllis, I know just the little hat you can wear with that". I said, "Well, I don't really want a veil". So she made me the sweetest little hat with gathered brown velvet onto net and I've still got it.

Mary Blyth
Fpr several years I went on holidays run by the Congregational Holiday Fellowship. I went to the Congregational Church. When I was 21 I went to France on one of the holidays with two friends, Janet and

Michael. Before we went we had a meeting with everyone going on the holiday.

When we were travelling to France, I h ad a very heavy case, and this young man offered to carry it for me. That was it, that was Ray, who would become my husband. By the time we cam back from that holiday we were a couple. He came from Wanstead in north-east London. Neither of us had a car, but he worked at the Ministry of Defence in London and we used to meet on Friday evenings and go to the theatres or concerts.

We were both living at home with our parents; we spent weekends at each other's houses. We went on holiday together in 1961 to Minehead. The first day we were there, we walked up North Hill and Ray proposed to me. I was a bit worried because from then on he didn't mention it all the rest of the holiday!

We were engaged for a year and were married in 1962. Our first home was a rented flat, in the Crystal Palace area of London, which was completely different to where we had come from. I think it did us good to go to this much poorer area and realised we had been very lucky in life. I think it altered us as people. The flat had enormous high ceilings and large rooms - it was that frozen winter of 1962/3. The way we used to keep warm was : we had a radiant oil heater and two armchairs and an old fashioned clothes horse. We used to sit in the two chairs with an old blanket over the clothes horse in front of the fire.

A year later we bought a maisonette in Bexleyheath for £2,995 with a mortgage of £17 per month. We both carried on working, but in 1964 I left work and had Richard, our baby, in 1965. On the day I had Richard, Ray had been before a promotions board and he was promoted and had an extra £1,000 a year which made up for me not working.

Troubles

Christine Kerswell

I must have been accident-prone when I was a child, because I seem to remember several little accidents. The first one I really remember was when I was about three and my grandfather had made a swing for me. It was hanging from the door of the wash house which was in our yard, backyard, and it was quite good except I had to go one better and I stood and of course, wallop I went, onto the concrete below and split my chin open. And I still remember my mother was in the middle of washing, she had her hair in curlers and a scarf on top of them. She just pushed, whipped, me into the pram and I was bleeding like mad and she ran round with me to Dr Beckett's house in Egremont Street. Went to the door, front door, and his stepmother came and said "I'm afraid Dr Beckett can't see you". Then he appeared and said "Oh, no, come in". He went into his surgery and I still remember he said "Your mother hasn't washed your face, it's dirty, I'll wash it for you". Obviously, he was freezing my chin. Then he stitched it. I also remember my mother getting a baking tin of fat, hot fat, from the oven. I came up underneath it, the whole lot went down my back. Once again, my mother rushed with me across the road, through the back way of Mr Gardner's chemist shop and Mr Gardner took me into the back room and put something on my back - what it was I don't know, but it must have been wonderful, because I haven't got a mark on my back, or a scar at all.

I remember when I was about two or three, my pet canary died. It was the first time I'd come across death because I went downstairs in the morning and found my canary on the floor of the cage. I didn't know he was dead. I thought he was just cold and I can remember wrapping him in the bottom of my nightie and taking him to my mother and saying "He's cold - I'm trying to warm him" and she just told me he was dead. I also remember that I had two bantams, a cock and a hen, in my backyard and I remember the rats got them. So that was my first brush with death. Talking of pets, I had a pet cat, Topsy. When we moved from Market Street to our house in St John's Road she went with us and we wondered whether she would stay or not. She didn't go away until we'd been there for a month and then she disappeared. They were still building the houses. It was a new estate and they were still building houses and we didn't know where she'd gone. A fortnight later I was coming home from school, at lunch time coming across the green which was central to the estate, I met a man called Walter Partridge, who used to be a gas fitter in Ely. He was carrying my cat. I ran up to him - I'd got a nerve because I was quite shy - but I said "That's my cat you've got". But he wouldn't let me take her. He said "Show me where you live" and he brought her home. She was so thin. He had been working in one of the empty houses. Gone to fit the gas and he could hear a cat crying. He traced the cries to the bathroom and he said to the men "There's a cat trapped here". They said "Don't be so silly, that bath panel has been on for a fortnight". But Mr Partridge said "Well, if you don't take it off, I'm going to lever it off". When they removed it my cat crawled out. Obviously, she had gone in there for the night and in the morning they'd come and fitted it in and she was trapped. Mr partridge had been taking her across to the mess hut to give her some of his lunch. She had survived a fortnight behind the bath panel.

In the 1947 floods, another of my memories. I had relatives at Sutton and we went to tea there and then we walked the top of the America and I can still remember the vast expanse of water, like a sea and seeing haystacks floating by and things like that. My mother had a friend who lived in Station Road at Ely near the river, and I remember the water seeping up through her floorboards, because the river was obviously overflowing in Ely.

Ann Powell

Military roads, you could pick those out in the fens, they'd go 'ba-dang-ba-dang' - they were made by laying concrete between battens of wood, the 'dang' you can hear is as you hit the wood.

A lot of these were made by Italian prisoners of war. In actual fact you say did it make any difference having the Americans here - it made a lot of difference having the Italian prisoners of war and the German prisoners of war. They were the ones who integrated. The Americans wanted the bright lights, they didn't want to come out to quiet fenland villages, they went to Cambridge and Newmarket. I won't say people didn't come into the dances in Ely from the villages but you must remember I was very small. I do remember the Americans quite well because my father used to take me to the cinema, first house, and we'd come home just I think before eight o'clock and I can remember coming down Forehill once and there was a fight in the *Baron of Beef* which is where Evans' mens' outfitters is now. There was a fight - you could hear the noise; up the hill roared a jeep, out of the jeep came the American military police with their white helmets. You must remember this was the blackout, but you could see their white helmets, they were also swinging night sticks - now I didn't see a night stick again until I was an adult so I must have seen this because they had these long batons that they were swinging. They dashed into the Baron of Beef and they came out and it was literally like a cartoon, they threw the men by the scruff of their necks and the seat of their pants into the back of the jeep, jumped in after them and roared away. So that is really all I can remember of the Americans.

The Italian POWs were up on Cambridge Road where the golf course is there now. They lived in Nissen huts which were really to homes for the forces when they came back. It was called the camp, it was quite well fenced but that didn't mean a thing because they used to spend more time on the outside of the fence than they did inside. In actual fact my father used to take them backwards and forwards to do work on the various farms and to do the roads as I described, and they were very jolly. I think they were rather pleased not to be in the war any more; they settled down quite happily here, they wore a peculiar brownish mauve battledress, they dyed the battledress and trousers into this peculiar browny-mauve colour. They had an orange or gold circle on the back of the top and on the knee of the trousers. So you pick them out from a distance. They went out to work on the farms each day and were for the most part quite good workers, sometimes they wanted a bit of sunshine, they found it very cold here, I understand. Once incident I remember my father relating was we have about the fens quite deep ponds, often they were where the gault was dug out and there's also places where gravel has been extracted, and this particular day was extremely hot and the Italians had been working presumably in the harvest fields or somewhere. Land work is extremely hard. I don't think people realise how hard work it is. But this particular young man he stripped off and dived in one of these ponds, now he died - the impact of the cold water you see, although the top foot or so of the water was warm, these ponds are so deep, that underneath it was cold and the shock killed him. This is quite a familiar thing now, but at the time no one quite knew why it suddenly killed him, and immediately the Italians wailed and moaned and I understand the foreman at the farm said, "Take 'em home Harry, we're not going to get any more work out of these today", and that's what he did, he brought them home presumably with the young man's body back to camp. It must have been very sad to have died like that so far from home when he thought he was safe.

I don't think, in actual fact, not only in wartime, we lived far better as far as food was concerned than the people, for instance, my mother worked for in service. Their meals were very mingy, I mean they'd have a watery soup, mutton and two veg. as you said, and a thing called a shape for their pudding, which I understand was a blancmange, and yet we would sit down to stew and dumplings and potatoes and vegetables and even now, I know you were saying you don't like the old meat and veg., as far as I'm concerned I still have almost exactly the same as my parents had because that's the kind of food that lines your stomach.

Terry Staines
My memory was probably the night on the day when my father died: I was twelve. I heard a lot of noise in the house, no one said what was going on, but apparently he died in the early hours of the morning from a blood clot. I refused to go in the following morning just to see him and I can remember sitting down just underneath the lamp just opposite the entrance to Little Lane and more or less all day I just sat there throwing very small stones at this lamp, very depressed. I wasn't allowed to go to the funeral for some reason, I don't know why this was and then I was sent with friends, a Mr and

Mrs Page who owned a butcher's shop in Newnham Street for a fortnight to live while my mother went to visit her sister and live at Sheffield for a fortnight.

The only illness I can really remember was sunstroke. I got that on a day trip to Hunstanton and remember one month in my mother's bedroom, oddly enough, because it had the least amount of sunshine during the day with the blackout blinds down and cold compress put on my forehead. Every hour the water had to be changed, every hour, and eventually when I was able to have a little light in the room, some friends of the family, Mr and Mrs Morris, brought a very large box of Rupert Bear books for me to read for the rest of the month.

Phyllis Trevers
I remember my mother-in-law saying that it was the middle of the 1914-18 War and a lot of soldiers were sent to that hospital. Granny Trevers used to go and scrub it up, clean it up. It was in Silver Street down the range. There's a big house now taken over by a lovely family.

No, no bombs were dropped. I just saw one Zeppelin but I don't know when. I'd have been about six.

My husband was called up when he was forty-five. I was married in 1938 at Little Downham. My husband come from Ely and he lived at the Crown pub in Silver Street. There were two Crown pubs in Ely. Old Mr Baxter lives there now. Just at the corner of Church Lane. Wilf went to war two years after we were married and he was away for four years. I came to Ely when I was thirteen - I don't remember much about the end of the First World War. One of my uncles came back and lived at Little Downham. I can remember the nurse going and dressing his wounds. He was shot in the leg.

Edna Nunn

I remember the floods, I was living in Cambridge then but I always went home at the weekend. This particular weekend they were broadcasting about the possibility of the Ouse bank going. It would either go our side and flood towards Ely or it would break the other side and go to Welch's Dam towards Manea that side and we were up this night waiting for the news bulletin. They were broadcasting all the time and telling where it went and they were advising our area to move upstairs against the possibility of the bank breaking. My father had been to a meeting at Downham Market, the other side of the Wash, and he wasn't home. We moved everything upstairs and in actual fact it broke the other side so that we weren't washed away or whatever. It broke at Welch's Dam I think, but there were other leaks, it flooded into Haddenham Fen.

I would imagine that my father would have taken [Teddy Barker] in our van [to hospital] because though I don't remember specifically how Ted got there, I do remember that our van was used for people who went into hospital and I can remember Ted telling me that when he was about seventeen he drove an old lady who was terminally ill with cancer in the van to Addenbrooke's.

Ted was brain damaged in that he was never able to go back to school. They took him back at March Grammar school but he wasn't able to concentrate. All his life he had this problem that he couldn't concentrate in adding up so that my father built him a garage and he had this natural ability. He helped in the business. In fact, he inherited the business but he didn't really make a go of it. He married and his wife was tremendously supportive. An Ely girl, Ethel Fenn. She was tremendously supportive and they had

three daughters. Because of my father's goodwill in the village he was supported by the village but it wasn't serious brain damage. It was just that he wasn't able to concentrate for too long.

It was shattering for my father whose one ambition was that Teddy should inherit. It may seem irrelevant but my father had left school at eleven. He'd won the only scholarship for a poor boy to go to the Derby Grammar school [but his father died and] he was sent to be apprenticed to a grocer and he started work at eleven. So dad's ambition was to make enough money to send all of us to a decent school. What happened was he sent his son to March Grammar school which was the best he could do and it was not wasted but...

I know that the whole of the accident - his treatment, his stay, cost [an awful lot of money] and what happened was the Crawford's traveller was visiting us at the business when Ted was brought home unconscious and he got Crawford's to back my father financially. That seems so extraordinary. Today it would never happen, it was only a small country business. But I don't think my father ever needed that money. He had invested money to educate us but that's why I went to Ely school because, fortunately, I passed the scholarship I went to Ely because his money that he'd got to send us to boarding school had gone. You see, he had a private nurse when he was at home. She lived in - another Mrs Pate from Guildacre Farm.

When he was getting better my mother and Teddy and Mrs Pate, his nurse, went to Southend. Goodness knows why Southend. It was probably the cheapest place. They went for a month and lived in a hotel there. My father had to pay for that. All his money went. He told me once that all his money went in getting Ted over this accident.

Maureen Scott

How are you supposed to feel when somebody close to you dies? How can you explain how you feel? Unless you are an extremely hard person you are absolutely devastated. It's something you never forget. Time may dim events but it doesn't take much to trigger your sadness again.

There were nine children on my father's side and nine children on my mother's side. With them and their descendants there has been a lot of funerals and they do not get any easier. One of the worst ones was in 1945, let me explain. Most weekends after school on a Friday I would cycle to my aunt's home at Prickwillow, returning home Sunday evening to get ready for school on Monday. The first Sunday in February '45 I cycled home as

usual; by 8 o'clock on the Tuesday morning an American bomber had ploughed into my aunt's bungalow, killing my little 19 month-old cousin and an evacuee sent to the country for safety. My aunt was on the danger list for weeks and had it not been for the RAF hospital in Ely, she would not have survived. As it was, she was in hospital for many, many months and always remained very badly crippled. My uncle was in a reserved occupation but had to work away, that was why I stayed with her a lot. I can remember dropping a posy of snowdrops onto the little white coffin. Now I have very few relatives left. As a child I was taught to stand still as a hearse passed and I still do this.

During the latter part of the war my parents did not impose restrictions on my movements to Hertfordshire. I spent a lot of time with my aunt and uncle who lived

M. Scott - Steam engine

on the edge of a wood between Woolmer Green and old Welwyn. The bungalow was quite large and she had a succession of evacuees from London. I had previously made friends with a very elderly gentleman who was very well known in the country for his carnations. Unfortunately he died, but he left me a beautiful cut glass powder bowl. At that particular time, the bungalow was full of pregnant ladies and before the bowl had time to reach me, one of them had broken it, without even saying sorry.

Another time it was a whole family - believe it or not, they were German - the very old grandmother could not speak a word of English. She went for a walk in the wood, a terrible storm blew up and she was lost. I remember feeling very proud as I was allowed to go with the search party, as the wood was my playground and I knew every nook and cranny, and guess who found her first. As it was only a short distance from London I witnessed dog fights on several occasions and of course, the barrage balloons and search lights fascinated me. I was not old enough to know any better. I have lots of reminiscences of this time.

I remember the floods again and my mother and father going to Southery - taking me obviously. We had to go a long way round because obviously we couldn't get on the normal route, and we helped friends in Southery move to a place in Norfolk, I can't remember where it was. They had to move everything that they could out of the houses into Nissan huts and that was a very traumatic experience for everyone.

My father was in the Home Guard and that did mean we could have several outings for some reason. I think he must have been lucky in the petrol stakes. So off we used to go. I can remember him taking me to Witchford, where in a large house in the centre of the village there was one of the foreign royals staying there; I also remember him taking me on a journey into Norfolk. I can't remember where. We went through some woods and small roads and it distinctly said 'No entry' but we still went and we came to this little track, took the motor bike and sidecar over this hole in the road and he stopped when we got a bit further. I thought he looked a bit sweaty. I said, "What's up?" And we realised we had just been over a bomb crater and the bomb was still in the bottom of the hole. So I've never forgotten that. The floods were, of course, the 1947 floods.

June Strawson

In 1933 I was four years old, only a very small child, but I can remember vividly, one night I was woken up by quite a commotion. And this was the fact my father had pneumonia and the doctor came in the middle of the night and I can see him now as I got out of bed to see what was going on and the doctor had his pyjamas on and that stood out in my memory and his jacket over his pyjamas and he came to see my father. And he said "Well, I'm going to use something I haven't used before, because we've got this business of the crisis coming up and I don't know about Mr Bent", as my father was called. He gave him an injection and it was the first injection that he'd ever given in all his years of practice and it really saved my father's life because he did get quite well, quite rapidly, after having that injection. Now I don't know what it was because I wasn't really old enough to know, but my father was 33 then and he lived to be 89, so really Dr Wilson in Littleport in 1933 saved my father's life. Diphtheria and scarlet fever were something that came to the villages and towns even in the country, every year, and we used to be absolutely terrified - didn't we Maureen? - of this ambulance, there was a very fascinating Fever Ambulance stationed at the Fever hospital in Ely and this horrible brown ambulance used to come and pick up children who had scarlet fever and diphtheria and they were very serious illnesses. We don't hear about scarlet fever now but I believe diphtheria is coming back; anyway, if you did get either of those diseases, you had to be isolated. And the Isolation hospital was up near Tower hospital, off the Cambridge Road [at Ely], and you spent about six weeks in hospital in those days if you had diphtheria badly. And I can remember I was only in the infant school and it would have been, Oh, dear, about 1935, one little girl in my class caught diphtheria and she died. And she was about six, well I was six as well at the time. And we had, at that time, the first immunisation against diphtheria so that was in about 1936, in this area, immunisation was given to the first lot of children. Then of course it went on for many years after that and still does, I believe.

At church we had a very notable, attractive in a country kind of way, a man called Joe Atkins. Now Joe Atkins was the undertaker. Well, Joe was absolutely marvellous, he was undertaker and he was the verger, so if you got married or had a christening or you died, Joe was always there. Now, this is quite serious really, because I think a whole lot of people in Littleport, dozens and dozens - more like hundreds - wouldn't have felt married if Joe Atkins the verger hadn't said the responses, and he was absolutely wonderful the way he said the responses. He didn't have a book, he just knew it all off by heart. Now when it came to singing, Joe was always just a little bit ahead of everyone else [laughter]. Now he used to get through the hymn and then he'd sing one line again and that's true.

And I can remember this undertaker he was then, he had these two hats, the undertaker and the verger, and he came into our house when my mother died, that was in 1947, and he looked at my father and my father had served his apprenticeship with him as a carpenter, so he knew my father from a boy. And he looked at dad and he said, "Rum old do, boy" and that was all he said, but that made a tremendous difference. There was a sort of calm air. I was in my teens then, and we were all very upset, but that did it. We knew because Joe had been and said those words he would do everything as far as the funeral was concerned.

Now of course we have funeral directors but they don't live in the village and it's all done so quickly, the bodies are removed immediately and I feel that death is all hurried now. You no sooner die than you're removed from your home, taken to a chapel of rest and then the church service comes later, but in Joe's day it wasn't like that at all. It was all given proper reverence and the body was kept in the front room. I'm sure some of you can remember that, and I can remember, it was the first death, close death, that I knew when my mother died, and I just went in and looked at her every now and again. Well, that wouldn't happen now. But I think that's a big change for the worse in a way, because you did get used to the loss. Those few days between the death and the burial in those days was eased over by the mourning. It wasn't morbid, there wasn't anything morbid about it, just got you acclimatised to it, so I think perhaps we have gone a step back now. I think that was part of dying and part of mourning, having the person in the house.

Lilian Martin
I was rarely ill and if I did feel unwell I wouldn't tell my mother because I didn't

55

want to miss school. In fact, I think I went to school with chicken pox and she didn't inspect the spots and I didn't tell her that I'd got any. I did, however, have to have a week off school when I was 13 and missed various lessons and never did catch up with them and I went to school with German measles and was grumbled at for going and a big rescue operation was formed to get me home because the school was 10 miles from home and there was no transport, and so my father's two elderly aunts who had a car and weren't safe to drive drove to Newmarket and it was a big adventure for everyone and they collected me.

We knew quite a lot about undertaking and funerals, because my grandfather was an undertaker of the old type and had a little push hearse, a little push trolley, and my father used to help with that. I do remember a very sad funeral, when a young boy - about 15 or 16 - in the very last days of the war, was shot by a stray bullet from a German fighter plane overhead. He was in the Air Cadets and went to a boxing match at Bury St Edmunds and on the way home a bullet, a stray bullet, came through the back of the

Martin - Collecting eggs

tarpaulin [of the covered lorry] and he was killed. I know my father and grandfather arranged this funeral and it was with full military honours.

I can also remember

we didn't have many pets, but we had a pet rabbit called Charlie Sam and he grew to an enormous size and eventually we decided we would kill him and eat him because didn't have all that much money, and I'd got a friend coming to stay for the week. So my father killed the rabbit and I was broken-hearted to kill it and my mother cooked it and then we set it on the t able and when my friend found it was our pet rabbit she wouldn't eat any but we tucked in, we thought we'd got to eat it, it was a nice dinner, so we ate Charlie Sam.

I can remember my grandfather dying in February 1953, and my uncle, who was no relation of my grandfather but my mother's uncle next door, died about two hours later. At the chapel, the Baptist chapel, the next morning there was a memorial service to someone else who had died and we sang 'Some day the silver chord will break'. I felt very, very tearful. The singing was not as good that morning as normal, normally the people at West Row sang in parts. The men all sat in the gallery, about sixty of them, and they sang bass and tenor. All the ladies sat downstairs and would sing soprano or alto. The singing always sounded lovely, but I can remember that particular day, the singing sounded dreary.

John Martin

This is John Martin again. I've got to tell you some of the little problems I had when I was young. My troubles and sad times began when I was ten, because my father died and we were then separated from our home. My sister went to domestic service and my niece had to go into an orphanage. She was only five at the time. That was a blow to me, losing - my niece and going away because my father had died. One of my brothers, Percy, Perce we used to call him, he went to live with my oldest brother named Will, Perce went to live with Will and his wife. Harry, the next oldest brother and his wife, took me in their home. I have forgotten to mention that until then I had been a rather weak child and suffered such illnesses as bronchitis, pneumonia, diphtheria, mumps and measles. This was apart from having my tonsils removed. With diphtheria I was taken to the Isolation hospital at Exning, which is near Newmarket. We called that the Fever hospital. I well remember going there in the ambulance and I well remember the sandwiches that we had, I didn't like them and I realised afterwards why I didn't like those sandwiches, because they were spread with margarine and not butter. We had always been used to butter and I know the difference - still do. This silly advert about Stork and you can't tell the difference. I could and I've always said I would like to be tested on that.

I remember coming home, the Reverend Owen, who was then minister at the Soham Baptist church, he brought me home ,and how I remember that was because he had a tricycle car, which was rather unusual, only well-to-do people had cars then. Rev. Owen had a tricycle car which was a small thing. It was named a Morgan; you have to be my age to remember a Morgan tricycle car.

Oh yes, and another problem of course was the school dentist. The school dentist used to come from time to time and he used to have a caravan in the school ground for a week and when one went to the dentist one went in this caravan. That was a bit traumatic in a way because the drill was operated by a treadle, which was similar to a sewing machine with the old wheel going round, you know, and I remember telling the dentist it was such a nice feeling when he left off.

Another sad thing in my life, that was when I was twelve, my oldest sister died

and she was the one who had brought me up as a child because as I have already said, my mother died soon after I was born, so my oldest sister brought me up. But when I was twelve, sadly she died. I shall never forget that feeling because I had never been to a funeral before and no one told me what to expect, and I had an awful feeling that when the coffin was in the ground I would see my dead sister's face through a window in the coffin. Of course, this didn't happen, but I've never forgotten that awful experience. Looking back, I'm glad I had such a good and loving family to look after me, soon after father's death.

Maureen Fresco

Although it's just an illness, the first memory of mine to do the doctors is when I was about three years old and I realise now that my younger sister was about to be born and I was sent to stay with my nana. I'd never stayed overnight there and I was a bit scared. She was a very old lady, she probably wasn't all that old; she seemed old to me, she had a humped back and a bun and my auntie Olive lived with her. All sorts of things were new to me there. They [had] an outside lavatory and we had sterilised milk. I'd never seen sterilised milk. I couldn't think what on earth this stuff was - it came out of a bottle and it tasted - cooked. That's the only thing I could think of - it tasted cooked. Anyway, I stayed there for about three or four days and she used to do my very straight hair up in papers. They were called 'crackers' to try and put some curl into them. There was never any curl, they just used to poke out at odd angles. Anyway, when I got home there was the new baby, nobody told me about this, there was suddenly this new baby there. So then there were three of us. Obviously, we had the usual childish ailments, I don't remember much about them but then I was about seven I suppose, I had measles and when anyone in the house was ill we had to walk half a mile down the road to the paper shop to phone the doctor. We very rarely had the doctor to us, it was too expensive, and we couldn't afford doctors, but when you had measles to had to have the doctor. So we came down - he came down - and yes, we'd got measles and it went through the whole house. One of the things we were always worried about was the 'fever' ambulance. Fortunately, we didn't have diphtheria or scarlet fever, or any of those things but other children in the street had them. And the fever ambulance would come along and red blankets and a stretcher would come out of the ambulance and we'd give the house a very wide berth!

Mary Turner

Think back to last week's childhood illnesses, I well remember that if a child of a fairly 'better off' family was taken ill and the doctors probably said 'keep her quiet', the only thing that used to surprise people was to suddenly find themselves walking over straw and it was strewn all over the road and all over the pavements. Everybody looked at each other and said "Who's ill?" because the horses that were left during the 1914-18 war - the best would have gone to the army - were huge farm horses and they drew tumbrel carts through the street and they made the most terrific noise you could ever hear and so the children, to be kept quiet, had to have the straw in front of their houses. And also, the other end of the age would be people who'd got an illness and elderly people who were still lying there in this hushed house with all the straw in front. Gardeners used to come out every morning, sweep it all up together to spread it all nice and evenly so that when the horses and tumbrels went past it was complete silence and we whispered to each other. I don't know what difference it made in the house but we were very

ordered on these occasions, tramping through the straw. The carts were so solid, they were built by the wheelwrights and carpenters and these iron-shod wheels were huge and made a dreadful clatter and I always remember that there was a blacksmith in our street. It was fascinating to me to see the horses being shod.

I thoroughly corroborate the talk about the 'ambulance', the brown ambulance, coming down the street and everybody was awe-struck at this terrible thing, that we wouldn't see the person anymore that was in the ambulance. But when I think about the outside toilets that we had to go in the junior school, you can understand that there was always this fear of diphtheria, and also another thing used to frighten us was consumption, which we don't hear about now. But in the big families, when they had lots of children, they must have been quite ill-fed and if this brown hut appeared in the garden, with a huge open window, and the poor children had to sleep in there all winter and you sort of thought we are never going to play with her again, she'll never get better, she'll die in that hut. So there were lots of sad things in those days and during the 1914-18 war was about the only time I can remember feeling ill and being so tiny they didn't take me upstairs in the cold bedroom, they had a fire downstairs and I had a little cot down there and somebody sat with me all night. In those days you had very green blinds, nobody had any coloured blinds in those days, and I can remember seeing tape on the window. They could see a light and they wondered why there was a light in the village at that time of night. So they had to put some extra curtains up.

Work

Ann Powell

I left the High School on a Friday in the summer and started work on the Monday as a Railway Goods clerk, in an office where the pedestrian crossing on Station Road now leads into the Tesco's site. The goods yard stretched over the whole site. There were vast sheds and railway lines leading up to the main line. In the office there were four women, eight men, the chief clerk and an office boy.

We stood at high desks with high stools and had round rulers which, if you left them on the desk, the slope sometimes ran them down and they dropped on your feet which was very uncomfortable. It was very male orientated atmosphere and, in actual fact, we had equal pay. What we did in the morning was to copy out the invoices that had come in during the night, for the various goods that were going to be - they hoped - on the shed later. And from the shed came each driver with a list

of what he had on his lorry for the various villages around. We then tried to match these with the invoices we'd already copied out and the delivery notes. If we didn't know a delivery note we had to quickly make one out. The drivers were often impatient with the girls in the office, and often teased them, sent them up. It was very much part of a working class attitude on the railway. If you belonged to the railway, you belonged to them for life, and even now, when I go back or if I meet up with any of those quite elderly men now, you are immediately on the same level with them and they joke and if they make fun of you, they like you. They don't bother with people who they don't like, they don't even bother to make jokes about them.

Terry Staines

I left Soham Grammar school at 16 years old to get a job. I could have stayed on as I had sufficient qualifications to stay on but the economic needs of the family were such that I had to leave because, simply, I

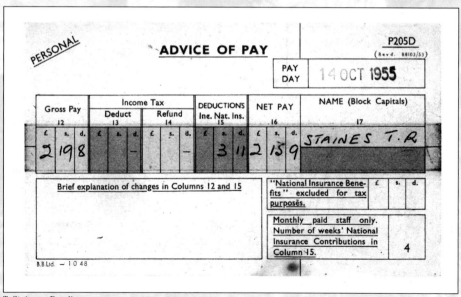

T. Staines - Payslip

had my mother at home on her own. I tried to become a policeman. I went to the Police Station and the route in those days was to become a police cadet and at that particular time they had no vacancies and so I was told there would be a vacancy in about six months' time. So I carried on with a part-time job working as a butcher boy working for Mr Page at his shop, Newnham Street. My mother was a regular attender of the Women's Institute and through that particular connection I knew a Mr Dickinson. He was the Assistant Head Postmaster at Ely and he asked me to come and see him one day and to see if I was interested in a vacancy for a male counter clerk at Ely Head Post Office and he talked me into taking what was then called the Civil Service entry exam for this particular job. I had explained to him that I was waiting for a police cadet vacancy to come up and he said, well, come along and see if you like it. You can earn some money in the meantime. I passed the exam and three months later I was offered a job at Ely Post Office. Another person also passed that same exam, but for a female vacancy, and she was to become my closest friend

for many years until a very sad road accident ended her life. Her name was Jean Wade and we worked together for a long time. In those days men were paid more than women for doing identical jobs and this gave her no pleasure at all. She was a far more efficient counter clerk than me and we both knew it.

Training initially was done locally and I was very fortunate I was trained by a lady called Kath Prior in 1955. We are still good friends and we worked in the post office together on and off for many, many years. After that local training I had to go to a place called Bletchley in Buckinghamshire, still surrounded in secrecy even in those days because it was the centre for breaking codes in World War Two. We had to be absolutely certain, we were forbidden to go in that particular area, and we had to be certain [not to enter an area of the park ringed by a tall wire fence], that we did not share the same meal times, break times or visit the same pubs etc etc and these people - it was all a bit eerie. While I was on my first training course at Bletchley, which was a four-week course, a policeman

apparently came to my house and said to my mother there was now a vacancy for a police cadet. Could I come along? Unfortunately, my mother said, without consulting me, he's got a job already, he's no longer interested. So that left me stuck, as it were, at the post office.

I worked at Ely until 1967 when the Head Post Office, as it was, was closed under a rationalisation programme and I was compulsorily transferred to Cambridge where I worked until 1995 when that, too, was compulsorily closed and I was transferred for the final month of my career to Peterborough.

At Ely I was able to walk to and from work and also lunch - I could also go home for that. To get to Cambridge I travelled by car, sharing for the first few years with Alan East from Ely and Norman Howe from Stretham, and as people left the service, finished up on my own. Then finally when I moved to Peterborough I travelled by train each day. In 1957 I failed the entrance exam, so to speak, for National Service. At the time they were taking A1, A2 and A1 plus and luckily for me I got grade A3 so I never did have to do any National Service.

John Martin

You've heard the expression "Truth is stranger than fiction". I am going to tell you something now that is quite true, you will never believe it, but this is entirely true. I am going to talk about tied houses. There used to be a system on the farm years ago, if one was a horsekeeper or a stockman you would live in the cottage that belonged to the farm and that was tied with the job, hence "tied cottage". It would mean that the person in charge of the animals would have to see to the animals, feed them, etc. on Sundays. We did not pay rent and therefore lived in the cottage rent-free but was tied to his job.

So if you lost your job, you lost your home, that was a disadvantage. I understand that since about 1970 things have been different. It used to mean that if you had a difference of opinion with the boss, a row with the boss if you like, one was without a job and without a home and they tell me that in the old days these farmers would tend to ring each other and say, "Don't employ him because he just left me". So a troublemaker? Yes! That was the disadvantage of that system.

Now this is the truth and this is what happened in 1950, at the potato harvest of 1950. My brother-in-law and myself, my brother-in-law was living in a tied cottage and I was free because I lived in a council house, but this is what happened to us. With the potato harvest there used to be groups, or if you like, gangs of ladies, they would be women who would be employed as casual labour for the potato harvest, about ten or twelve women in a gang and they would also be employed for singling sugar beet, or the beet harvest. Now sometimes these ladies would be paid more than the men because they were casual labourers - so much for the equal opportunities - the ladies were getting more money than the men. On this occasion, when my brother-in-law and myself were working together, the women were being paid £1 a day and they worked from 8 a.m. until 2.30 p.m. for £1. My brother-in-law and myself were getting paid 15s.8d. which is about 79p - we worked from 7 a.m. until 4 p.m. - do you get the idea? - so it was what we might call a double whammy, not only were we working longer hours, 2-1/2 hours a day more, but also we were getting less money. We did this for about a fortnight and my brother-in-law said, "This is not fair. I'll have a word with the boss." Well, he didn't see the boss but the boss's son, and explained the situation and he said, "Now John and I have agreed that we would be willing to work the extra hours providing we were paid £1 like the women. We will still work the extra 2-1/2 hours each day", and this fellow said, "Well, I shall have to see the governor" (who was his father), which he did. The next day my brother-in-law said to him, "Have you agreed about the money?" and he said, "Yes". What did father say? Father said, "You go back and you tell those men they need a job in the winter" and that was it. The impression was, y'know, we weren't working in the winter; of course, we were working in the winter and he wasn't going to pay us extra anyway but we wanted a job in the winter, these women were casual workers and would go elsewhere and that was it. Now this is the real truth, believe it or not, the truth is stranger than fiction.

June Strawson

I can remember as a teenager taking part in potato picking and it was quite a hard job - in fact, it was a very hard job. I used to go with my mother as my mother's work was helping grandad get the potatoes up. I used to help her to do her 'rech'. Now this word 'rech' I think must be a fen word because we don't know how to spell it. It was the amount of the row of potatoes that each woman had to pick, the distance, that's right, the length, yes the length that you had to pick up. In between the machine, which was called a spinner that went round the field and you had to get your 'rech' done before the spinner got back to your part and the men [who] were working on the potato picking day, they used to throw up the cobs. Now the cobs were the baskets the the women picked their potatoes in and they had a hard job too because they went all the way round to the whole length of the field you see picking up the cobs, so this business of potato picking was a horrible job in a way because it was always in the autumn. In those days we had a potato picking holiday, it was war time you see and we were given about a fortnight in late September and early October to do this potato picking and it was damp and the thing that stands out in my memory was the very damp mornings, all the land was damp and the potato tops that were picked up seemed to be hanging everywhere and it was a very horrible job. It could be foggy and then very often, of course, the sun came out and it was a lovely day for the latter part of it but it was very hard going for these women. I think we still had horses then - it would be about 1944 or something like that. It would still be horses, wouldn't it - I think Grandad still had his horse called Punch. Cob catching was another job and as you say, young boys often did the cob catching for a time but it was too hard work for them to go all day, wasn't it? So the potatoes were then carted off the field in the horse and cart and put into clamps, great heaps that were then covered with straw and then earth to protect them from the frost, waiting to be sold to the potato merchants. The fens were very famous for their potatoes and of course, they still are, but it is a very different business today. They kept very well and the best ones were King Edward's.

Margaret Springer

My friend's mother suggested perhaps that office life wasn't for me and I would like to do my nursing training, which horrified my mother who felt that to work in an office with a safe job I would be OK and didn't think I had the qualities to be a nurse. I went to Addenbrooke's hospital and had my interview. I didn't really have enough qualifications but Miss Ottley, the then matron, was very kind and said I could start off if I could pass my prelim (examination) that would decide it. Leaving home was quite simply because I went to start in 1954 and lived in the nurses' home in Croft which was an amazing experience as I had been an only child at home and now I was with lots of other girls.

Phyllis Trevers
[I left school when I was] thirteen, nearly fourteen. In the summer holidays my mother came into Ely to Miss Howard on the Downham Road. She had a servants' registry. I went there and she had a vacancy coming up with Mrs Lloyd of the Palace Green Cottage. My mother thought [it] was the answer to a maiden's prayer because the Revd Marner Lloyd had been the clergyman in her village of Witchford.

So I was duly taken to see Mrs Lloyd and "Oh, Florrie, Florrie" she said to my mother, "fancy seeing you!" So mother said "I've come because Phyllis has just left school and I want her to get a living-in job because we haven't got a very big house and the boys are still at home". So Phyllis was accepted and offered five shillings a week and her food.

[And this was in 1925] So I was taken up to see a little bedroom with a sloping roof and a window overlooking the Ivatts who lived at 25 St Mary's Street. I thought "Ooh, that's not bad". There were some lovely trees and flowers and so I said "I think that will be all right mum". It had a little bed, a dressing table, which was a box standing on end with a fancy curtain round it and this mirror, and on a side was a bowl and jug for me to do my washing with and a bucket in the box underneath for me to take along to the bathroom with my water in when I'd finished my ablutions. So Fanny, the mistress was called, accepted me. She had two nieces, they were very kind and helped me so I was duly taken into Esslin's shop in the High Street in Ely and I had a morning dress which was blue. I had morning aprons which had a bib on and I had an afternoon dress which was black, and white fancy tea aprons which I had to change into to take the tea in.

Edna Nunn

Yes, we finished work at 12 o'clock and I caught the train from Cambridge to Ely up until the war. My brother or father would come and meet me. There was a bus but I had to wait till 2 o'clock. That was until the war came and there was petrol rationing and for several years I either waited for the bus or got to Black Bank station and walked 2 1/2 miles.

Working for the Ministry of Transport I had the idea that if I could get the authority for my father to have petrol to collect me it would be all right. Well I was superintendent of the Sunday school. Do you remember Ron Bircham, the clergyman?

Well, he was leaving and he asked my mother if I would take over the Sunday school. I tell you who was in my top class - Alan White. I applied to the office that issued petrol for private cars for half a gallon a week for me because I was superintendent of the Sunday school. I got it. So after that my father would collect me from Black Bank station and take me back.

Next year, the war started and from 1940 we were often working seven days a week, twelve hour days. We were preparing for evacuation from East Anglia, getting all the vehicles, all the furniture removers had their vehicles ready to make into buses with forms so that they could evacuate all the people. There were military people working with us but we were in control. We got the sand and gravel organised for the aerodromes in East Anglia. People like the fairground people, we were organising them with tipper lorries to carry sand and gravel. They couldn't read or write so we had the problem of trying to persuade them to abide by the rules. They appreciated what we did because the fair came to Cambridge once and my friend and I went round and one of these fair people recognised me and she said "You come and have a ride, duck". And we got on the chair-o-plane and she wouldn't let us off. She said "No, ducky you have a good ride!"

My father had some land. His idea was to buy land and become a farmer. He had this great ambition. My brother was helping the harvesting with a man who worked on the farm and coming back with a load of straw my brother was on the top and he fell off and the two-tined fork penetrated his head, eye and nose, so he lost the sight of one eye but it broke the cranium and the piece was piercing the covering of the brain.

He had a fantastic operation to remove that but the operation caused slight brain damage. When my brother had the accident the man who worked on the farm was so terrified. He removed the fork from his head and was too terrified to tell my father what had happened. Ted came home unconscious. I can remember him being carried in unconscious and he lay in his bed unconscious for a fortnight until the doctor ordered him into hospital. They'd no idea. Eventually this man admitted what had happened. I can remember living in Cambridge with my mother and he was moved into the Evelyn Nursing Home because that was quieter, they felt. They felt that he needed quiet. I can remember going to visit and the grass was allowed to grow. It hadn't been cut because of Teddy and my mother said, "That's because Teddy's so ill and you must be quiet when you go to see him".

Peter Kerswell

I left school in 1953 and my life was entirely different yet again. In north-west Durham where I lived the main industry was the mines, the Consett Iron Company. Of course, there was the ship building on the River Tyne and also on the Wear at Sunderland. But my father would not have me going into anything like this. He was a miner and he said "No way do you go down the mines!" There were three boys and none of us went down the mine. I thought "What am I going to do?" So my very first job was milk-boy and I used to deliver the milk around the streets. Of course, the old way was by horse and cart. Well, the first month wasn't too bad because the chap I worked with and the round I covered was around where I lived. Then I moved from that round at New Kyo to the Catchgate round and I didn't I find the difference. The Catchgate round was spread out further and also there were two chaps. The chap in charge of the round, we never did hit it off from the word 'go'. A clash of personalities. All of a sudden I was off carrying two baskets, metal baskets of twelve bottles of milk each which wasn't too bad in the summer but in the winter it was a different story. This particular area I went to was called Loud Bank, but it was a hill. It wasn't too bad carrying two crates of milk but as the families got bigger I had to take more milk. Ronnie, my boss, would take the

horse and cart and dump off three crates of thirty-six bottles of milk and I was having to deliver three sorts of milk - homogenised, pasteurised and sterilised and there were gill bottles of orange drink, then cream. It was a nightmare. You have different tokens for each milk at the Co-op - north-west Durham Co-op - and on top of that you had to collect money for the single and double cream - it was quite something. Then I went in the summer of '54 on the 'heavies'. These were lorries which used to deliver [to local diary depots in north-west Durham, and from these depots the milk was delivered to households].

John Martin

Just one or two amusing stories that may or may not be true, but quite amusing really. Talking of the potato harvest, there was one occasion when the ladies were quite busy picking up the potatoes. Some would pick them up with both hands and some only one. This Mrs Drage (?) was only picking with one hand - one man went to her and said "Come now Mrs Drage, scrape them up with both hands" (I'm talking in fenland now). So she said

"Huh! Seeing I only get paid with one hand, I'm only going to pick potatoes with one". Another amusing story was that this tractor driver had got a trailer and the women used to ride on the trailers sometimes and he was going to a place called Burnham - I think that's in Norfolk. I'm open to question there, always pronounced 'Bunham' in the fens. So someone stopped him and said, "Where are [you] going with those old women then?" He said, "I'm going to Burnham" and he said, "Hang on a minute. I'll go and fetch my old girl and you can burn her as well". When I was a lad working on the farm the horse keeper said to me one day, "Go back to the stables and bring me a horse. I want another horse, I want to change horses". "What horse shall I bring?" So he said, "Bring the white-legged 'un". Well, apparently there was a horse there, it was a bay horse but it had white legs, he didn't tell me this, he just said, "Bring the white legged one". I came back with a white horse, so he looked at me and said, "Huh, you've got the wrong one. I told you to bring the white-legged one". I said "Well, it's got white legs, hasn't it?" He wasn't at all amused at that. The last one for now, it's when I used to collect eggs for the Egg Marketing Board, several years ago. I used to go to a man in Earith and he was complaining about his hens. He said,

"These hens don't lay at all" so I said, "Oh, dear". He said, "No, most disappointing, they will not lay but I'll make them lay". So I thought to myself, perhaps he's going to give them some chemicals, which used to be used in those days, a chemical called Ovum which was a stimulant used to help the chickens to lay. Y'see I thought he was going to say that. He said, "I'll make em lay". I said, "What are you going to do then?" He said, "I'll cut their legs off. They'll lay then. They can't stand up".

Celebrations

June Strawson

Now get back to more cheerful things. Now we don't call it fair in Littleport, we call it Littleport Feast, and I think it goes back to the time when the patron saint of Littleport was St James, although our parish church is now called St George's. The Feast of St James was the time when Littleport Feast took place, or fair, and the people who [owned the fair] were called Thurstons and they came to Littleport. I don't know if they do now, but they came all my young life and they came through my mother's childhood and my grandmother and grandfather met at Littleport Feast or fair, with the rides and things, and I can remember as a small child, we'd be taken down to the fair. It was on for nearly a week, three days to a week, depending a bit, and there were stalls and rides on the Gas House green. Now the Gas House green is really the centre of Littleport. I don't think it's even called that any more. I can't remember what it's called - Ponts Hill? That's right, yes. It isn't a hill, it's a flat space, but that's typical, isn't it?

Anyway, the fair used to arrive and they'd been coming for years. We all knew the fair people. We knew which stalls they were on and I remember at one time we even put up one stall-holder and her husband and she had a rolling, penny-rolling stall. And I can remember I was allowed to go down to the fair, everybody went to the fair, and I was allowed to have so many pennies to roll down, and she said to me and my mother before we went down, now go away when you're winning because she said we always get it. And I have never forgotten that. I feel a bit mean sometimes, because if I win anything anywhere I always keep it, and I think that was through this fair-lady from Thurstons fair all those years ago in the 1930s.

Now the magic of the fair was when it got dark, because the lights came on everywhere and the electricity was made by steam-engine in those days, called a showman's engine, an enormous engine that used to stand outside the fish shop, which was [Scarborough's, then] Cross's in those days, don't think it's Cross's now, but for a long time it was and the electricity was made there, and on one occasion I can remember we had a cake-walk. I think it was cake, or cape, I never knew which (cake walk). I only just remember that, that's right, going backwards and forwards, you've got it, yes. Well, that was lovely. The swing-boats and all those sorts of things.

And there were crowds and crowds of people all the time. They had stalls all the way from Ponts Hill, the complete length of Wellington Street, both sides, and they went round the corner into what was really Station Road, as far as the Turk's Head. Now the Turk's Head has been empty for years and years, but it used to be a very thriving inn in the old days, and the Turk's Head was where the pottery stall was, the china stall, and I still have three jugs that came from that stall. Now they're nothing to write home about, they were only fair jugs, but it was something that was done. The women used to love to hear the men talk on the stall. He'd got these bargains and all the chatter, and he'd reduce things and reduce things till it was almost a give-away business, but I expect he still made a living, but that was part of the thrill of the fair, or the Feast, as we call it.

Christine Kerswell

1973 was a very important year in Ely. It was 1300 years since the monastery was founded by St. Etheldreda. One of the first things was 'It's a Knockout' which was held in the park and Ely triumphed over Hartford. I think it was, and they went on to win the I don't know what it was, the international thing, anyway. They won everything that year. There was a lovely day in the summer when all of the schools in the area came into Ely and spent the whole day in Ely and there was no traffic in Ely at all. The whole day was spent in games and dramatics and anything connected with the past and all of the children were in costume. The school that I was at, which was Littleport County Primary, we decided to do the Viking raid on the cathedral; every child in the school was in costume which was quite an undertaking because we had between four and five hundred children to dress. They were dressed as Saxons, Vikings, nuns, monks and animals. I was in charge of dressing the nuns, seeing about making the nuns' costumes. Some teachers went to a warehouse near Wisbech and bought bales of cloth quite cheaply, and then, having designed the costume we had battalions of nuns in and sewing machines going like mad in the hall, and eventually all the costumes were made. A big Viking boat was constructed on a trailer in the school hall, from wood, and Viking helmets were made from balloons and papier maché swords etc were made.

On the day, everything had to be into Ely by 8 a.m. so the Viking boat was brought in on the trailer, a low-loader had to be in by 7 o'clock because after that the whole of Ely was closed to traffic. The children all bussed in and luckily it was a really fine day. I don't know what we would have done if it had rained because we lunched in the Bishop's Palace grounds and there were too many children to go into buildings, so luck was with us, the gods were with us you might say.

All schools pageant was acted out on St Crosses Green and the Viking boat appeared to music of Mars in the Planet Suite. We did it several times throughout the day. We were worried about children getting lost, and somebody hit on the idea of the person in charge of the group holding a yellow flag so Littleport school had a whole lot of yellow flags on broomsticks and the idea was, that if a child got lost from its group, all they had to do was look for a yellow flag and join onto that, and luckily we lost nobody. It worked.

Later on that year the Queen came to Ely and the children were asked to go into Ely dressed up in costume but obviously it wasn't hot then, they couldn't act outside so they had to stand on the Market Place and wait for the Queen to appear. It was too cold for the children to wait outside so we waited in the Rex cinema until it was time for the Queen to come and then we all went out and waited and she came around. And I remember she spoke to several of the children, and afterwards they said "She said the same thing to us". She said to everybody "and what do you represent?" So it was a really memorable year for Ely.

Lilian Martin
The famous Saxon Mildenhall treasure which is in the British Museum was discovered initially by Mr Butcher of Holywell Road when he was deep ploughing in West Row. He called his employer, Mr Sid Ford of W.J. Ford & Sons, Agricultural Engineers, who was a keen amateur archaeologist. They carefully dug up the treasure and cleaned it up and because Mr Ford thought it was pewter Mr Ford displayed it in his display cabinet. It was sometime later that it was declared treasure trove and both men received a monetary reward but it was a close thing as the find should have been

declared immediately it was found. They faced possible fines or imprisonment. The wife of the young couple who moved in to our cottage next door was the daughter of Mr Ford and she would have taken me to her father's house whilst the treasure was there. I can vaguely picture the polished wood case with glass fronts and the items inside and expect it was the Mildenhall treasure. West Row was a good area for finding flints and primitive tools. I have a few. My uncle had a large collection of flints, coins etc and these are in Moyses Hall Museum, in Bury St Edmunds.

May Turner

I am still in the years 1930s when I was living in Ely, and I always remember this event very clearly. Through the grapevine we heard that Queen Mary was coming to visit the Cathedral. So we got permission to go across the Palace Green and we got as far as the gates of the Galilee Porch

and we just stood there for a little while. There was no special service going on. The Cathedral was not celebrating anything, there were no floods and no marching soldiers or anything to show that something was happening, but we, when we saw the Queen get out of her car and walk across the pavement as close as I am to you and with her was the Duchess of York. That was our now Queen Mother because Queen Mary was still the Queen. She was very tall and very straight upright and regal but it was her make-up that rather spoilt her because I suppose they tried to take some of the age from her, that the make-up was so heavy she could not smile, she never smiled. Her face never slipped but I can always remember the six little kiss-curls she had across her forehead. The toque kept them in place and she always wore the same type of long coat, with long reveres and of course, in the winter it would be furred, but this was a lovely summer day and she had plenty of lace floating around, and also, all her strings of pearls which kept her head up, about six of them, very tight round her throat, so that she was entirely different from the dear little Duchess of York who was dressed in the loveliest palest pink. The pink that you get inside the shells and of course she was bubbling over with excitement, laughing at everybody and waving, and I've never forgotten that experience because nowadays people forget what Queen Mary looked like.

Then later on there was the abdication coming into the 30s and whilst I was at Dr Bamford this happened and I remember being asked if I would like to come down and listen to it. [Tucking up the sleeping babe, Mrs Bamford and I walked into the dining room.] The doctor and his friend naturally got up and then we all stood there, more or less to attention because it was the King who was speaking to us and we had to listen very carefully and I think it was so sad to think that this one man could give up his crown, his throne, his country, and all the people who loved him for the sake of this one woman. It seemed incredible to me but at least the tension was going out of what we were listening to because we knew then that all this argument about whether he should be crowned or whether he should leave the country was at last settled and we could then get on with our lives, but it really was incredible that it should happen like that. That's it.

Phyllis Trevers

I also remember the two Queens coming to Ely and I was working in Egremont Street, and I thought "Fancy, two Queens coming to Ely", and "How can I see them?" So I threw down my duster and I raced down Egremont Street and got to the Cathedral just as the two Queens were coming out and my husband was very secretive about his work but he knew they were coming and there he stood, well, he wasn't my husband then, he was my boyfriend, there he stood taking pictures of them, and of course I told him a thing or two when we met, and anyhow, that was my experience of seeing the two Queens which they made great publicity of. And another occasion, he had to go to Ely station and photograph Chamberlain, he was the Prime Minister I think, and so of course he - I - got a first close up of Chamberlain coming to Ely station then, I thought that was very good.

And when the floods were on I met royalty in the Peacock. We were, I think, the Women's Institute, we were doing sandwiches and what not for the flood people. I think it was the Duchess of Gloucester and the Duke and they came into this hall and shook hands with us all. Well, you never wanted to wash your hands after that.

Edna Nunn

I didn't go up to London in 1951. At that time I was working in Cambridge at the Ministry of Transport. 1951 was also the Spithead Review and because our office was really run by just girls (all the men were called up) and we were given the privilege, just a few of us were allowed to go on board ship in the Spithead Review. I was one of the lucky ones that was picked to go on a merchant ship. It sounds so exciting but in actual fact we were moored off the Isle of Wight and our ship swung round with the tide and all we ever saw was a Russian submarine and every so often it came up and they stood up on deck and with our binoculars we saw the Queen come round in Britannia and at the end of three days my eyes were on stalks.

Mary Blyth

On the day of the Coronation I was lucky enough to win one of the places on the Embankment that the London schoolchildren had. We went from school as a group and we had to meet very early in the morning to get to London and the teachers found our allotted places. I remember that we had an ice-cream, they came along with ice-cream and a drink. I was fifteen by now and we just saw the whole of the procession as it went towards the Abbey and it was lovely to think you were there and it was happening. Everybody remembers the Queen of Tonga. Then we went home and we watched the main event on television. We had a television in our house. In fact we had a television in our house through the war. It wasn't working but my father had bought a television before the war so we were able to watch plenty of things.